Y0-AFT-481

LITURGICAL PRELUDES

LITURGICAL PRELUDES

BY

MOST REVEREND LUIS M. MARTINEZ, D.D.
Late Primate of Mexico

Translated from the Spanish

by

Sister Mary St. Daniel, B.V.M.

THE PETER REILLY CO.
131 NORTH THIRTEENTH STREET
PHILADELPHIA, PA.

Nihil Obstat

JOSEPH A. M. QUIGLEY

Censor Librorum

Imprimatur

RT. REV. MSGR. THOMAS F. MCNALLY, P.A.

Vicarius Generalis

Feast of the Maternity of the Blessed Virgin Mary, 1961

Library of Congress Catalog Card Number: 61-18859

Acknowledgments

Quotations from the Scriptures are from the Douay version of the Old Testament and the Confraternity of Christian Doctrine revision of the New Testament, as published in *The Holy Bible* by P. J. Kenedy & Sons, New York.

Liturgical quotations are from the following sources as indicated in *Notes*:

Roman Breviary in English, Copyright by Benziger Brothers, Inc., New York, N. Y., 1951.

St. Andrew Daily Missal, Copyright by E. M. Lohmann Company, St. Paul, Minnesota, 1958.

A Short Breviary, edited by William G. Heidt, O.S.B. Copyright by The Order of St. Benedict, Inc., Collegeville, Minnesota, 1954.

In memory

of my parents

Daniel and Ellen Tarrant

THE TRANSLATOR

FOREWORD

In Catholic circles, the name of Archbishop Martínez, late Primate of Mexico, connotes immediately the terms theologian, spiritual writer and sacred orator. The present volume reveals the prelate as a discerning and devoted liturgist.

Liturgical Preludes presents a series of spiritual reflections on the ecclesiastical year, season by season. It is a devotional book based on solid dogma. Though antecedent to *Mediator Dei,* it harmonizes perfectly with the teaching of that Encyclical. The author regards the liturgy as 1) a school of the spiritual life, 2) the glorification of Christ, 3) a prelude to heavenly beatitude.

Part One, "Purity in the Liturgical Cycle," treats of purity in its broad, positive aspects. God is Purity; pure souls mirror God; they understand the divine language. Part Two, "Lights on the Liturgical Cycle," reflects His Excellency's luminous, penetrating contemplations on the liturgical feasts and seasons.

The key to Archbishop Martínez' spiritual doctrine may be found in three themes predominant in his writings: purity, love, suffering. *Purity* gives spiritual vision; this divine light increases *love*; love is satisfied only by *suffering* for the beloved.

In *Liturgical Preludes* we meet the mind of an experimental mystic, whose writings are colored by his awareness of the supernatural phenomena within his own soul. The work is replete with original, unique and inspiring viewpoints.

The recent initiation of the process of beatification of Archbishop Martínez will delight the thoughtful reader of his works.

SISTER MARY ST. DANIEL, B.V.M.

Feast of the Nativity of the Blessed Virgin Mary
September 8, 1961

CONTENTS

PART ONE

PURITY IN THE LITURGICAL CYCLE

PART TWO

LIGHTS ON THE LITURGICAL CYCLE

Part One

PURITY IN THE LITURGICAL CYCLE

ADVENT

The Feast of Purity

ADVENT

Chapter I

THE FEAST OF PURITY

The feast of Mary's Immaculate Conception invites us to meditate on purity, that heavenly flower which, through Jesus' exquisite care, has been acclimated to our arid earth.

To comprehend perfectly what purity is, it would be necessary to comprehend perfectly what God is, because purity is either God Himself or the reflection of God in creatures.

The blessed, contemplating God face to face, are impelled to repeat unceasingly that canticle of purity, "Holy, Holy, Holy," the supreme praise of love heard in vision by Isaias and by St. John.[1]

God is purity because He is what He is. His nature contains nothing of earth, nothing of the creature. His divine simplicity excludes all composition and mixture. He is an infinite, indescribable reality. Though possessing the whole wealth of perfection, the entire plenitude of being, and all the splendor of Beauty, yet He is ineffable Unity and divine Simplicity.

His interior life is the expression of His purity. The divine Persons are ever multiplied through His infinite fecundity. His purity maintains, and we might even say, confirms and consummates the inconceivable purity of His infinite and most simple Unity. The Father is the Purity without beginning, who through His fecundity engenders the Word, the Purity of Light — "Light of light," as the Church calls Him. From the Father and the Son proceeds by divine fecundity the Holy Spirit, the Purity of Love, who by an inexpressible bond of union consummates Purity by completing Unity.

But why speak of divine mysteries with stammering lips? Our intelligence can scarcely grasp the idea of purity even in its negative aspect—what it is not. It excludes the created and the earthly. When we want to look into the positive reality of purity, that ocean of light dazzles us completely.

If to be pure is to lack the earthly, how can that heavenly flower live here where everything is earthly?

Light, being diffusive by nature, spreads even over the mire. This contact does not stain the rays, for when reflected from the unclean surface, they emerge unmixed with the mud. Rather, the light brightens, illuminates and adorns the mire with the colors of the rainbow, and like the rainbow, having embellished the dirty pool, it is reflected in a splendor untarnished by anything earthly.

"God is light,"[2] says St. John, because He is purity, truth, and an inexhaustible fountain of happiness and of love. That indescribably diffusive light is shed upon the universe, penetrating all beings and illuminating them with divine splendor, yet without mingling with them, without losing its infinite simplicity and even communicating to them all a reflection of its splendor, a participation in its whiteness. It shines even in darkness and the darkness does not envelop it.

Light readily penetrates objects which do not emit light themselves but which permit light to pass within. The crystal, because of its perfect transparency, thus becomes a veritable reservoir of light. It is the same in the spiritual order. Souls, like crystals, have an immense capacity for light. The Creator made them marvelously receptive to its beauty when He impressed upon them "the light of His countenance,"[3] a reflection of divinity. The "true light that enlightens every man who comes into the world,"[4] can penetrate souls even to their very center, giving them a celestial brilliance, and embellishing them with divine shades of color up to such a point that, before the magic of that light, the impurities of creatures disappear, so to speak, just as the indefinite outlines of the crystal disappear when the glory of light bathes and enfolds them.

Only spirits are properly capable of purity because only they are capable of light, susceptible to divinization and conversion into pure reflections of infinite Truth and eternal Love.

Even in the natural order, souls (restricting ourselves to them and leaving out the angels) have an immense capacity for light. In their very essence is graven the image of the Trinity like a seal of royal race, like a vestige of the divine breath, like a germ of light and of purity that can be changed into dazzling splendor.

But the supernatural order, which is the divine order, perfects and increases to unsuspected immensities the spiritual transparency of souls and makes them capable of an incredible purity because it makes them sharers in the nature of God.

Grace elevates souls to the lofty, rarefied regions in which, like eagles, they can fix their gaze on the eternal Sun and plunge into the fire of infinite love without being burned. These are not vain words and sterile hyperboles. St. Peter teaches us that through Jesus Christ we are partakers of the divine nature: "through which he has granted us the very great and precious promises, so that through them you may become partakers of the divine nature."[5]

Like children who play with precious stones without suspecting their value, we carry costly jewels in our souls without appreciating our treasure. Through grace and its accompanying gifts, the soul is transformed, divinized — do we know to what degree? To the degree in which our intelligence has the same object as the divine intelligence: God such as He is in Himself; and our will the same object as the divine Will: God possessed in Himself. Our spiritual gaze is fixed upon the very ocean of light where the divine eyes rest; one and the same fire of love burns in the Heart of God and in ours, kindled, so to speak, by the ardor of charity and the action of the Holy Spirit.

Why does God love souls to such an extent that the Father gave them His Son, the Word became flesh and died for them, and the Father and the Son sent them the Holy Spirit as the gift of Their love? Only because souls bear in their essence that divine image which God desires to attain its full and most blessed perfection.

When grace reaches its plenitude in a soul, everything earthy seems to have disappeared from it. So perfect is its transparency and so complete the penetration of infinite light that, although it keeps the indefinite profile of the creature and vestiges of its origin, all this disappears, as it were, before the divine outburst of light. In a fine, clear crystal nothing is seen but the penetrating light; so in the soul the divine eyes no longer see what that soul is, but only the Lord Himself, most faithfully photographed in the soul's clear, polished surface.

St. Paul must have had profound insight into this divine

transformation of his soul when he gave expression to this victorious, heartfelt cry: "It is now no longer I that live, but Christ lives in me."[6]

"The soul in a certain way becomes all things," said Aristotle. The pagan philosopher did not come near suspecting the broad compass of his highly significant principle developed to its ultimate consequences by the genius of St. Thomas Aquinas: through grace the soul in a certain way becomes God.

It requires thought to discern even faintly how the soul can have purity despite its earthly, created status, and especially how it can eventually reflect that divine perfection in such a way that the creature characteristics seem to disappear in the plenitude of its divinization.

Two criteria are helpful in judging the degree of purity: to look downward and to measure the distance that separates a soul from the earth, or to look upwards and observe its nearness to God, for purity is both alienation from the earthly and participation in the divine. Both the one and the other correspond exactly.

Mortal sin, venial sin and imperfection are the terms of comparison for forming the stages of the purity that rises from the earth; the degrees of charity, the virtue uniting us intimately to God, express the degrees of purity that ascend to heaven. As all the virtues and gifts increase in proportion to charity, any of these habits could serve to form the celestial ladder.

Millions of souls have ascended it, and millions have reached its blessed summit; but even the greatest saints see, away down, at the base of the ladder, some sin, at least original sin with which we are all stained. The saints also carry even to the heights of sanctity the dust of certain faults, very light, indeed, and indeliberate, but faults, after all, from which no one can be totally free without a special privilege from God.

Mary alone never saw her soul's purity darkened with the dust of any stain, nor did she see in any part of her triumphal course toward heaven any sin or trace of worldliness. By a unique and singular privilege from God she was preserved from original sin from the first moment of her Immaculate Conception; by another privilege derived from the first, the Lord did not permit her ever to be stained even with those unavoidable failings of human weakness.

The base of that mystical stairway of Mary's life is set in purity and in sanctity. Who could suspect the treasures enclosed in that unique purity, which knew nothing whatever of earthliness, which was born in light, and which never needed to be purified and transformed because it came from the Most High, pure, immaculate, lovely? Mary's purity was the most perfect reflection of Him Who is "the whiteness, the fairness, of eternal light"; it was the stainless mirror which reflected from the very beginning the kindness, the beauty, and the purity of God.

Let us not think that the purity which adorned the Virgin Mary from her conception was merely negative; no, from her first instant Mary's soul was divinized by an exceptional, singular participation in God's purity. The grace that Mary received in her conception surpasses unspeakably the sanctity that the saints attained after long years of abundant graces and of marvelous fidelity; therefore, the Church applies to Mary those words of Scripture: "The foundations thereof are in the holy mountains."[7]

Chosen souls select as their ideal of sanctity the heights of Mary's holiness and unique purity, inferior only to the purity of Jesus' soul, hypostatically united to the Divinity.

Only the eyes of God can penetrate those depths of purity which Mary received in the first instant of her existence and which deepened indescribably in the long years of her life. Gifted with a wealth of copious and exceptional graces, Our Lady cultivated them with an exquisite and complete fidelity.

Let us venerate in loving silence Mary's celestial purity, and let us ask her to bathe our poor souls with the reflection of her divine whiteness, stainless as mountain snow gleaming in the sunlight, and flooding the dark, gloomy valleys below with the reflection of its immaculate fairness.

CHRISTMAS

The Fecundity of Purity

CHRISTMAS

Chapter II

The Fecundity of Purity

The feasts of the Immaculate Conception and of Our Lord's Nativity are closely intertwined by a divine logic. The first is the feast of purity; the second is the feast of the fecundity of purity. God made Mary so pure in order that she might become the Mother of God, and she became the Mother of God because she was so pure.

Our feeble intelligence can scarcely catch even a faint idea of the profound bond that unites purity and fecundity; but illumined by the Light of God one begins to see, though imperfectly, that fruitfulness is the expansion of purity, that a being is so much the more fruitful as it is the more pure and that to infinite purity belongs an infinite fecundity.

Divine Fecundity

God is purity, "God is light," and that Light, eternal and infinite in its mysterious extension, engenders another Light, the divine Word, whom the Church calls Light of Light, who is the Light of wisdom; and from the unbegotten Light and from the engendered Light proceeds, by a new mystery of fecundity, the Holy Spirit, Light of Love, whom the

Church calls "lux beatissima,"[1] most blessed light, light of bliss.

The mystery of the Trinity, which is the mystery of purity, as the blessed proclaim in their eternal Trisagion,[2] is also a mystery of fecundity, because it is a mystery of purity. All creatures, according to their beauty and perfection, display a trace of divinity; therefore, a sparkle of purity and of fecundity shines out from them.

True purity, however, the image and participation of God's purity, is found only in the supernatural order. On this level, fecundity also touches the boundaries of the infinite, so to speak, because its end is always divine.

SUPERNATURAL FRUITFULNESS

True fecundity in souls always produces Jesus as fruit in one form or other. The divine Word is the fruit of the eternal fecundity of the Father.

How meager the fecundity of souls in the natural order compared with that divine fecundity. The genius of Plato bequeathed to us his immortal Dialogs and the mighty Stagarite. What a book and what a disciple! It is the best that a noble soul could produce through its own spiritual fecundity; but although that book is converted into an inexhaustible fountain of wisdom and that disciple is perpetuated in a glorious school, can that fecundity be compared with fruitfulness which has something divine for its end: *Jesus?*

It is true that even in the natural order souls may produce a likeness of the Word of God; a book, if it contains the truth, is a reflection of eternal Truth; a disciple who receives from the Master the treasure of wisdom is a figure of the infinite Wisdom who receives from the Father the treasure of the divine essence.

But what in the natural order is a similarity and a figure turns into an image and participation in the supernatural, divine order. In this order the fecundity of souls has as its end not a likeness of the Word, but the Word Himself, Jesus, "who has become wisdom and justice and sanctification and redemption."[3]

In order to understand this divine fecundity in the supernatural order it is necessary to plumb those words of the Apostle St. Peter: ". . . through the knowledge of him who has called us by his own glory and power — through which he has granted us the very great and precious promises so that through them you may become partakers of the divine nature."[4]

The divine nature is what it is by its very essence; it admits of no compositions; it is purity itself. The divine Being is most pure because He is what He is; His thought is most pure because He is fully known only to Himself and in knowing Himself He knows all things; His love is most pure because He is loved infinitely only by Himself and in loving Himself He loves all things.

Through grace souls share in that purity in such a way that their supernatural operations have the same object as the divine operations; in the order of grace, the basis of all knowledge is the knowledge of God and the foundation of all love is divine love. In the measure in which the soul progresses in the life of grace, the greater is its purity. Its thoughts and affections keep concentrating more intensely upon God up to such a degree that, on the heights of perfection, the soul thinks only about God and loves no one but Him. It focuses all its thoughts upon that divine thought alone and coordinates all its affections with that divine love.

If the thoughts and the love of a soul are thus pure and God-orientated that soul cannot but produce divine fruit. The Holy Spirit, a fountain of purity, is also a source of fecundity; what could the fruitfulness derived from Him produce but Jesus only?

There is no other fecundity in the supernatural order than the one producing divine fruit: in Bethlehem, on the altar, in souls, Jesus is ever being born, reborn, and growing up until He reaches His maturity.

In the Scripture Jesus receives this mysterious name: "Oriens"[5] — the one arising, the eternal renewal — and in truth, He is forever being born: in the Bosom of the Father, in Mary's womb, in the hands of His priests, in the interior of souls. And He is always born of purity, either infinite purity or purity communicated by the Holy Spirit.

The Father in the expansion of His purity, in the splendors of sanctity, engenders His Word, in that unique instant which never ends. "Thou art My Son: this day I have begotten Thee."[6]

MARY'S FECUNDITY

The mystery of the divine fecundity is reproduced in time in the womb of Mary, possessor of the greatest purity after God Himself. In the manger of Bethlehem the astonished world contemplates the fruit of the virginal fecundity of Mary, the Word of God garbed in our Flesh, conceived in the splendors of purity. "Conceived by the Holy Ghost, born of the Virgin Mary,"[7] fruit of the Purity of heaven and the purity of earth. "The earth has borne its fruit,"[8] too, and that fruit is the Fruit of heaven itself.

An echo of the eternal word of the Father resounds in the immortal cave; the Virgin on her knees adoring in an inexpressible transport of tenderness and abasement can say to Jesus what the Father says to Him eternally: "Thou art My Son; I have given Thee birth today."

SUPERNATURAL FRUITFULNESS OF THE PRIESTHOOD

After Mary's fecundity, there is none comparable to that of the priest in the most solemn hour of the Eucharistic sacrifice. After Mary's purity, there should be none greater than that of the priest. Every altar on earth is the reproduction of Bethlehem as well as of Calvary; every day the priest re-lives both the joy of Bethlehem and the sorrow of Calvary. Every day, by virtue of the sacred words, the very One who descended into the Virgin's immaculate womb descends into the priestly hands. Jesus is born in the pure Host, so to speak, to be sacrificed, as He was born in Bethlehem to be immolated on Calvary. The thirty-three year cycle of fecundity of Jesus' life is retraced upon the altar in a few moments, for time signifies very little in the eyes of God, "For a thousand years in thy sight are as yesterday, which is past."[9] That cycle is love born of purity and buried in pain; one might say that the entire mystery of fecundity is enclosed in that triumphal course.

The priest possesses the marvelous power of reproducing Jesus in the Host and in the chalice; he possesses also the no less marvelous power of reproducing Him in souls. Because he is a sacrificer, he stands sponsor for souls, with a paternal relation that is above all created fatherhood.

St. Paul experienced deeply the delightful transports and the unspeakable sorrows of that priestly paternity. He calls those whom he has evangelized "Little children"; the expression of a heart-felt conviction, a profound reality. With his usual audacity he expresses for us the basis and the nature of that spiritual fatherhood in which he glories. "For although you have ten thousand tutors in Christ, yet you have not many fathers. For in Christ Jesus, through the Gospel did I beget you."[10] For the Apostle, to be the father of souls is to give them to Jesus, it is to reproduce Jesus in them: ". . . My dear children, with whom I am in labor again until Christ is formed in you,"[11] he writes to the Galatians, explaining to them the mystery of his paternity. The Epistles of St. Paul would serve well as a study of that spiritual paternity which made him feel the joys and the sorrows of his children. He carried them in his heart,[12] they were his joy and his crown,[13] none of them could suffer without his suffering, nor be made to stumble without his being inflamed.[14]

If not all souls can aspire to St. Paul's perfect, unlimited apostolate, all can and should share in it to the extent and in the form pointed out to them by their providential mission and the place they occupy in the Mystical Body of Christ, for all should cooperate in building it up mightily.

SUPERNATURAL FRUITFULNESS IN THE CLOISTER

Jesus is formed in us not only through the priestly ministry and external activity but also by souls hidden in silence and obscurity. Perhaps we should say that such souls especially reproduce Jesus, for supernatural fecundity is proportional neither to the eloquence of the word nor to the activity of the work, but to the interior of the soul.

Wherever there is a pure soul, there is a Bethlehem and a Calvary, there is an altar for the mystical sacrifice of love and of suffering, and there is a bountiful fruitfulness that bears Jesus and diffuses Him secretly in souls, like an invisible radiation, charged with an astonishing efficacy.

How many wonders wrought upon this earth originate in the stainless purity, the secret sacrifice, and the hidden yet irradiant love of unknown souls whom the eyes of men will never discover, but whom the eyes of God behold with utmost complacency!

The world does not understand it. Enemies are scandalized at those enclosed gardens, seemingly sterile, where the Church guards her virgins. "Let them alone; they are blind,"[15] we can say to the foolish ones in the words of the Master. The very Christians who are filled with admiration at the self-denying maidens who nurse the lepers or teach children the doctrine of Jesus do not begin to understand the inexhaustible fruitfulness of contemplative souls, because they do not know the secret of the apostolate. Perhaps earth does not have more fruitful places than those gardens of roses and lilies, for in them purity is cultivated and from purity sacrifice and love are born.

SUPERNATURAL FRUITFULNESS IN THE WORLD

Souls can be fruitful, for even in the midst of the world they can be pure. Anyone can aspire to share in Mary's blessedness and happiness by causing Jesus to be born in self and in the hearts of others. When a woman extolled the

Virgin Mary because she was the Mother of Jesus, the Master spoke these profound words: "Rather, blessed are they who hear the word of God and keep it."[16] Commenting upon these words St. Bede the Venerable said:

> The Savior graciously gives his approval to the woman's testimony, saying that not she alone was blessed, who merited to give birth to the Word of God according to the flesh, but all they also, who, by hearing the same Word, and conceiving in faith according to the spirit, strive by good works to bring it forth and, as it were, nourish it either in their own hearts or in those of their neighbors. For the Mother of God was blessed indeed, in that she gave flesh to the Word of God in time, but still more blessed, in that she ever keeps the same word in her love, throughout eternity.[17]

And so it is that all supernatural fecundity produces Jesus as its fruit; this most excellent fruit stems from purity. Each degree of purity has its own degree of fruitfulness.

At Christmas, the feast of fecundity, Holy Church celebrates with three liturgical Masses the three principal divine fecundities; the fecundity of the eternal generation of the Word, which belongs to the infinite Purity of the Father, in the third Mass; the mystical fecundity of souls, which belongs to created purity, in the second Mass. The first Mass celebrates that unique fecundity of Mary, who, though a creature, seems to touch the boundaries of the divine, since her unique purity is midway, as it were, between the purity of all other human beings and infinite Purity itself.

In mystical fruitfulness a wide range is discernible, just as there are innumerable degrees of purity effected in souls through the abundance of God's grace and the fidelity of the recipient.

Only in heaven shall we be able to contemplate in its splendid beauty that gradation of apostolic fruitfulness, which is in proportion to virtue; but if we consider now not each individual soul but its category in the Church of God, we must say that the richest harvest and consequently the greatest purity belongs to priests, who possess the stupendous Eucharistic power and perfect paternity in souls. After the priests in this mystical hierarchy come the virgins and those pure souls who, eager for purity, sacrifice and love have renounced the world to consecrate themselves with eternal bonds to the sweet Spouse who feeds among the lilies.

PRESENTATION

The Oblation of Purity

PRESENTATION

Chapter III

The Oblation of Purity

On Christmas Eve we contemplated the divine fecundity of purity, for on that most sacred night, as the Church proclaims, the blessed Virgin Mary "losing not the glory of her virginity gave forth to the world the everlasting light, Jesus Christ our Lord."[1]

But that night was a beginning rather tha a consummation. In it was initiated the era of peace and of love foretold by the prophets, the true golden age predicted by the Sybil, the "new order of time" of which Virgil sang.

The divine fruit of Mary's purity is the jubilant love that appears upon the earth, prepared to run its course with gigantic steps; it is the dawn that rises from the depths of the sky and which from splendor to splendor will reach the fullness of noon-day.

What can be the goal of that triumphant course of love? What will be the zenith of that divine Sun? . . . Sacrifice, Calvary, the Cross. That Lamb of God, who takes away the sins of the world comes to be immolated; that Sun which rises in the midst of the joy of heaven and earth comes to sink in a sunset of sorrow.

The Divine Child is scarcely born when His eyes seek Calvary, His Heart sighs for the Cross, and full of loving impatience, He is offered by Mary's virginal hands forty days after His birth as a victim for sacrifice.

The feast of the Purification is the Offertory of the Mass to be completed on Calvary; it is the loving oblation of heaven's all-pure One made by earth's purest one.

This feast is the fulfillment of the ancient Law; it is also its completion. Jesus is redeemed with legal offerings according to the Mosaic rite; but He is also offered as the divine reality that comes to complete the figures and the ancient types. During many centuries the ancient rites had predicted "the salvation of the Lord" now announced by the old man Simeon. Holding in his arms that Child who is "a light of revelation to the Gentiles, and a glory for thy people Israel,"[2] he seems to unite both Testaments in his faith, his hope and his love.

Mary made that most pure offering not only because she was the Mother of Jesus, but also because she was the Immaculate, and only earth's supreme purity could make the oblation of heaven's Purity.

To comprehend the mystery of this oblation it is necessary to study the intimate relations between purity and sacrifice; it is necessary to know that in the designs of God purity is destined for sacrifice; that the latter is not acceptable and fruitful if it is not encompassed by virtue, and that love is the divine bond that closely unites purity with suffering.

The union of purity and pain is expressed with pleasing symbolism in the Canticle of Canticles: "As the lily among thorns, so is my love among the daughters."[3] Purity is an exceedingly fair, fragrant lily having a mystic affinity with thorns.

There is a purity that comes up from the mire, that

struggles against all that could stain it, that combats in the midst of earthly lowness until it rises victorious to live in the regions of light, like a white-plumed dove that pulls itself loose from the hunter's snare, shakes off the dust of the earth and flies away to the heights. Such is our purity; stained in its origin, imperfect in its luster, fragile in its preservation. In order to be pure, we need to be purified; to keep ourselves pure, we need exquisite care; it is ever necessary to burnish our whiteness; we never finish erasing the marks of our sad origin.

Our purity needs pain to exist, to be preserved, to be perfected. Only suffering purifies, and only anguish whitens and shines. Outside of sorrow nothing in this corrupted world keeps the fragile flower of our purity unstained; it can fade at any instant. Our purity is a lily that blooms among thorns; it needs them as an encircling protector. Only among thorns can the lily display the snow of its petals and scatter the wealth of its virginal perfume.

Suffering would not purify, nor would it preserve and polish purity, if it were not the instrument of love, if it were not love itself. When love contacts this world's wretchedness, it is transformed into suffering, just as a heavenly flower transplanted to earth would lose color and perfume in this heavy, stifling atmosphere.

There is another purity marvelously and singularly preserved from blemish by the devoted care of the Divine Gardener. It is a purity that never struggled, that never knew the earthy, that always lived in light. Like the snow of the heights, it descended from heaven and, far from fearing the mud of the low-lying valleys, it lavished upon them the splendid reflection of its immaculate whiteness. This is the purity of Mary.

To Our Lady especially is applied the expression in the Canticle in its true interpretation. In the midst of souls, comparable to dry and prickly thorns, Mary, like a spotless, fragrant lily, stands out among them all.

In another sense also that pregnant expression of Scripture is applicable to Mary, for that surpassing lily lived among the thorns of anguish. Purity cannot live on earth without sorrow; one would say that its atmosphere is sacrifice and when this is lacking, the lily languishes and, changed into a very delicate, virginal aroma, it emigrates to heaven.

I scarcely dare to speak of the interior sacrifices of purity, of the suffering that envelopes it, of the thorns among which it lives. It seems to me that I am lifting uncautious veils, taking shy secrets by surprise. My poor word is not worthy to touch mysteries that only the angels of God can approach with exquisite delicacy.

The most superficial — and yet the deepest — of the afflictions of Our Lady's purity was, without doubt, to live among the thorns of this corrupted world. As the dove sent out by Noah returned to the ark because it found no place to alight upon the water-covered earth, so Mary, holy and immaculate, must not have found a spot to rest her foot upon this sin-deluged earth where everything bears the trace of sin, — for even inanimate creatures groan for the liberty of the sons of God; — where it is necessary to live among so many stained or mediocre souls. We are able to live here, but she? And not because she might fear being contaminated, no; but on account of the revulsion that the less pure produces in a heavenly soul. An angel exiled from heaven might have suffered less upon contact with the earth than Mary Immaculate, who is purer than the angels. Pure souls live isolated because their surroundings are not in harmony with them; still more, they live in torment, because the extreme sensitiveness of their purity seems to be wounded by the gross contact with the worldly atmosphere; their clear gaze perceives the deformity of evil everywhere; their refined hearing suffers from the perpetual discord of the world; their impressionable heart feels oppressed by narrow human egoism. Poor Blessed Mother! What interior martyrdoms she must have endured! Her soul's comfort was to find near her one formed to understand her, the singularly purified soul of Joseph. She found consolation in Jesus especially, true heaven in which she took refuge from the world for thirty-three years.

Purity undergoes still more subtle martyrdoms; by a divine instinct this virtue is hidden even from its own gaze, as if afraid of its own beauty. To all purity belongs a modesty; supernatural purity always bears a very delicate, spiritual modesty. Holy souls rejoice when their limitations are discovered, but they do not tolerate having their virtues noticed. They are right, the reason is evident! This divine modesty is not to be analyzed, for one never dissects the sublime; but if we were to discover its elements, we would see that this virtue is formed of humility, purity and love combined by a mysterious formula whose secret God has reserved to Himself.

The Gospel lifts the veil hiding this divine shyness on one single occasion, when Gabriel announced to the Virgin the stupendous Mystery. Mary was disturbed, "troubled at his word."[4] That perturbation which enamored the God of heaven was the martyrdom of the purity that feels itself discovered, the unspeakable modesty of the soul that is embarrassed at its own beauty. And who knows but that while the angel was speaking, divine eyes penetrated the depths of the Virgin's purity, an inexpressible affection enraptured her soul, a delightful kiss of love made the Mother of God tremble with happiness and with trustful timidity.

The purity of earth is destined to be united with the Purity of heaven; it yearns for Purity as the spouse longs for her chosen one, as our poor heart craves the infinite with unutterable aspirations. The deeper the love and the more ardent the desire, the more intense, the more delicate, the more torturing is modesty. The soul would like to hide itself from that beauty which it longs for, and to be far away from that infinite Purity in which it desires to be engulfed. Only God could say which martyrdom is more rigorous and more dreadful, the martyrdom of desire or that of modesty; only God could say which is the greater, the desire of union or embarrassment at the divine possession.

Let us not continue profaning deep mysteries with shallow words. Let the blessed Mary and pure souls guard the secret of the King and let it suffice for us to praise in silence the works of God as we understand faintly that love is the golden thread uniting happiness and reserve, purity and its matchless martyrdom.

Surpassing the purity of Mary is that of Jesus which, not having room in the sacred Humanity, is scattered throughout the world like a rare perfume that passes through the containing vase; such is purity in its divine plenitude, in its amazing superabundance, poured out everywhere, saturating the world, purifying and beautifying all creation. The purity of Jesus, unlike ours, does not fear contact with the world, nor does it hide from it, like that of pure souls. However. Jesus' purity feels even more than His holy Mother's the horrors of the corrupt world; it is a triumphant purity that walks over the mire giving it the whiteness of snow, that passes through the world cutting off the thorns among the lilies; it is a productive, redeeming purity which transforms the arid earth into a paradise of purity. Ever since that heavenly purity appeared upon the earth, whitest lilies have not been lacking in the garden of the Church. Among these the Beloved recreates and then He transplants them to the heavenly garden; He Himself calls to the South wind and the North wind to scatter the aroma from His Garden, until the day of time declines and the shadows increase in the solemn, somber passage of the centuries. . . .

But Jesus' lily, more than any other, grew among thorns; the thorny pricks suffered by all pure souls including Mary, are neither so sharp nor so cruel nor so deep as those that transfixed Jesus' most pure soul and immaculate Body. Our Lord's exterior suffering, and especially the interior, are unparalleled, just as His love and His purity are without peer.

The impetuous breeze of love scattered the fragrance of that purity throughout the world to perfume and to purify it; but upon contact with the world's wretchedness, the purity and the love of Jesus were changed into tremendous suffering. A law established by God on this earth requires that if love is to purify, it must come from purity and then be converted into pain. In heaven, the law of fecundity is that love spring from purity and in purity be consummated with eternal joy; the Word comes from the Father and returns to Him through the Love that proceeds from Them; but on earth, Jesus was born of Mary, earth's supreme purity, to complete His triumphal career of love and of fecundity on Calvary. There stands the Cross, which includes all griefs and ignominies, because it bespeaks the utmost of purity and of love. Jesus had scarcely left Bethlehem when His purity met Calvary through His Mother's oblation. The sweet Babe whom she carried in her virginal arms to the temple was an alabaster vase that would imbue the world with fragrance; that vase was to be broken into a thousand pieces to scatter the divine aroma. That mystery of sorrow accomplished, Mary's heart also would break with an anguish foretold to her at the Purification by the last prophecy of the Old Law.

The purity of Jesus was destined for martyrdom because it was destined for fruitfulness; it would redeem the world; it would shine as the light of the Gentiles and the glory of Israel.

Everything connected with divine sacrifice must be pure. Even on Calvary, the Virgin Mary, mother of Priest and Victim, stood at the foot of the Cross. On the day of the Purification she offered to God the oblation of Purity.

In sacrifice, no less spotlessness is required of the priest than of the victim and the altar; all should be equally stainless and therefore, strictly speaking, neither on Calvary nor in the Mass is there any priest, victim or altar other than Jesus Himself. The supreme participation in the first Mass, — and in a certain sense, the only one, — that of Calvary, belongs to Our Lady by virtue of her incomparable purity.

That purity, which appeared in the world on the feast of the Immaculate Conception and produced its fruit at Christmas, made its holy Oblation on the day of the divine Child's Presentation in the temple.

For these reasons the Purification is the feast of priests and of victim souls, of those who share in the official priesthood of Jesus and of those who share in His mystical priesthood. We priests offer the bread and wine whose substance will be changed into Jesus through the omnipotent efficacy of our words; victim souls offer themselves to be changed mystically into Jesus by the mystical transformation. Jesus is always the holy oblation, the Immaculate Host. Consequently, the oblation should always be made by purity; to make the offering, one should be like Mary. What purity is required in priests! What purity in victim souls!

All sacrifices have the same law because all are renewals in miniature, so to speak, of Calvary's surpassing sacrifice. The mystical sacrifice of the real Body of Christ offered upon the altar and the real sacrifice of the mystical Body of Christ offered in the interior of souls should trace the same sacred cycle: *love* born from *purity* and consummated in *suffering*. . . .

LENTEN SEASON

The Immolation of Purity

LENTEN SEASON

Chapter IV

THE IMMOLATION OF PURITY

With inimitable mastery and charming simplicity Holy Church presents throughout the liturgical cycle the admirable series of Jesus' mysteries, like the strophes of a divine poem of purity, love and sorrow.

The Christmas cycle, full of joy and of hope, blends into Lenten austerity and Passiontide grief through the oblation of purity in the Presentation, for the Incarnation was prelude to the Redemption, and the most holy Babe of Bethlehem is the Lamb of God who comes to take away the sins of the world.

Oblation logically becomes immolation, and the dolorous stages of the latter unfold gradually in Lent, Passiontide and Holy Week — divine pictures of Our Savior's immortal drama which should be renewed mystically in souls.

Septuagesima prepares immediately for Lent. It depicts the deplorable state of humanity amidst the shades and shadows of death, eager for the light of life to illumine its path, and longing for ineffable purity to blot out its faults.

The immolation of Jesus began in reality with His mortal life and continued throughout; He endured it in the depths of His Heart, hidden under the veils of divine silence, simplicity and admirable serenity. Mary's pure, loving eyes could not actually fathom that deep, interior mystery of sorrow. Joseph's prudent glance, perhaps, could scarcely discern that immeasurable abyss.

To understand Jesus' interior immolation it would be necessary to penetrate these two extremes: His purity and the iniquity of men; it would be necessary to understand the mighty outburst of pain produced when these two incompatibles were fused in the Sacred Heart by an incomprehensible love.

Purity, like the column of fire that guided the Israelites, is both light and darkness; light for the heavenly-minded, darkness for the earth-bound; joy for God, horror and bitterness for the sinner. God hates sin infinitely, because He loves Himself infinitely. His purity is both infinite love and infinite horror; and because it is horror, it brings immense suffering to the reprobate. If God were not infinite purity, heaven would not be so delightful nor would hell be so terrible.

All purity is just like that, because it participates in eternal purity. In the proportion in which a soul possesses purity, it has a loving inclination toward God and a horror for sin. The greatest suffering a pure soul can experience is the approach of evil; therefore, there have been saints who fainted away upon hearing the name of sin.

There is no purity like that of Jesus, and consequently, no horror for sin like His. The hatred for sin — which in God is infinite but without suffering — is immense in Jesus by reason of the hypostatic union; and on account of His human nature, so exquisitely sensitive to suffering, it is sorrow, bitterness and immolation.

Jesus' ineffable purity was in contact with sin for thirty-three years, not with one sin only but with all the sins of the whole world; not from afar, but closely united to them; not like something alien, but in a certain sense, as if those sins were His own; because ". . . the Lord hath laid on him the iniquities of us all."[1] Who can comprehend the dreadful meaning of this Scriptural sentence? With even greater audacity, St. Paul says: "For our sakes he made him to be sin, who knew nothing of sin, so that in him we might become the justice of God."[2]

That is, the purity of Jesus, totally foreign to sin, was laden by God with our sins so that we, sons of wrath, might be justified in Jesus.

But only God knows the immense horror, the unspeakable suffering and the indescribable confusion that this strange fellowship of sinlessness and sin produced in the Sacred Heart. The Scripture speaks of the sufferings that beset the holy Victim as "the sorrows of hell."[3] Obviously infinite purity projected upon sin as justice and as hate produces hell; but when that ineffable purity contacted the world's sins to take them away, what could result but an abyss of suffering in Jesus' ever spotless soul?

What humiliation for Jesus to feel Himself responsible for all our iniquities! What a struggle in His Heart between love for His Father which made Him abhor sin, and love of mankind which impelled Him to cover our guilt with His perfection and His pain! Here is the secret of our Redemption as well as the mystery of its deepest dolors. Rightly did Jesus present to St. Margaret Mary Alacoque His thorn-torn Heart wounded by a spear, surmounted by a cross!

During the years of His hidden life, Jesus' immolation was interior; but at the beginning of His public life, He desired to trace, one by one, every stage of exterior expiation.

First, He wished to expiate our offenses by forty days of

solitude and fasting; afterwards He humbled Himself to the extreme of putting Himself in contact with the Evil One and undergoing that which is closest to sin, temptation.

Neither the devil nor sin could make Him waver, but the one and the other must have horrified His spotless purity.

Those enemies vanquished, others were awaiting Him. The public life of Our Lord is regarded as a masterly sway of light and a triumph of power and of love. In truth, it was all this; but it was also an immolation and a struggle.

As the hand of Jesus touched the leper, the paralytic and the corpse, His purity contacted sorrowfully all the sin and the loneliness of the men among whom He exercised His divine apostolate. When in the presence of pitiable wretches possessed corporeally by the demons, He experienced the same unspeakable horror He felt upon the approach of those repulsive agents and instruments of Satan: the priests of the Synagogue, the Scribes, the Pharisees, that is, pride of authority, of learning and of spurious virtue. The struggle against these enemies was bitterly cruel to the tender-hearted Master.

Parallel to the magnificent unfolding of Jesus' doctrine, which would have its divine epilogue in the Cenacle and on Calvary, there developed also during the three years of Jesus' public life, the terrible, sacrilegious conspiracy of His enemies, which would end bitterly in treason and in deicide.

Two progressive phases appear in the liturgy of Lent and Passiontide: one, a poem of light and love, the other, a drama of darkness and hate; both exquisitely artistic in their magnificent exposition, both living through eternal verity revealed rather than veiled by the divine transparency of symbols; both so human that they reach even to our innermost heart, yet so divine that they come impregnated with the unction of the Holy Spirit.

The Church knows well how to show the gigantic struggle between sinlessness and sin, the abyss of suffering carved out by eternal love as a burial place for the sins of the world!

On Passion Sunday when the statues are veiled, we feel the dire conspiracy closing in upon us; in the palm procession our heart feels a joy mixed with sadness at sight of the Master's seemingly ephemeral triumph, prelude of suffering and death. The matins of the Sacred Triduum with their moving ceremonies seem like the final effusions of the Redeemer's love upon which is projected the somber figure of the traitor.

Holy Thursday, illuminated with the splendor of the Eucharist, filled with the immortal echoes of the discourse at the Last Supper, so sweet, so sad, so divine, so human, so simple, so profound, so loving, so sorrowful: Holy Thursday, with its tender washing of the feet, for the Church does not wish to forget one single detail of the Cenacle; the day on which she scatters flowers as a sweet reminder, as a seal of gratitude, as a most delicate proof of tenderness; Holy Thursday is the day of love, of an exile's love which bids farewell, which weeps, which is immolated, which seems plunged into the depth of all wretchedness and which, nevertheless, is more powerful than death.

Good Friday is the day of sorrow, of immense desolation, the sky covered with darkness and the earth trembling with fright. The day of the Cross hides beneath its dreadful appearance, infinite love and earth's only happiness. In the Mass of the Catechumens the Church has found the fitting pattern for expressing great sorrow with victorious love, deep desolation with heavenly hope, death so terrible with life so abundant. It begins in silence which, on a sudden, is pierced by an impression of most poignant grief; the remembrance of Israel prepares for the inimitable melody of the Passion, simple as truth, austere as sorrow, and deep as everything divine is deep. Then, the triumph of the Cross disposes souls to adore the sacred Host elevated quickly above the altar like the divine ray from a sunset of suffering and of glory. That Mass would be a masterpiece of art if it were not something better: the cry of sorrow from the most tender heart of the Church, possessor of deep understanding both of divine things and of the innermost secrets of the human heart.[4]

Guided by the teachings of the Church through its admirable liturgy and the interior action of the Holy Spirit, souls ought to penetrate, to feel and almost to live, during these holy days, the unutterable sufferings of Jesus, immense as man's iniquity, the justice of God, and the love of His Heart. Souls ought to venerate and love that purity which, impelled by divine love, is transformed into inconceivable pain for blotting out the sins of the world.

But it is not only the purity of Jesus that is immolated; there is another similar purity, united to it indissolubly and sharing in its redemptive mission: the purity of Mary.

Since the day of the Purification, the Mother of Jesus bore in her sensitive, immaculate Heart the germ of interior suffering. In Nazareth Jesus must have cultivated that blessed seed with His affectionate confidence, for He must have poured into the only heart that understood Him well the loving sorrow overflowing from His soul. Could that intense, hidden anguish of her Son possibly escape the intuition of Mary's purity — mirror of Jesus' purity — and of her virginal yet maternal love? Could the Son be immolated and not the Mother?

As the features and even the emotions of one who looks into a mirror are faithfully reproduced, so in Mary's spotlessness the love and the grief, the joy and the sacrifice of Jesus' purity are reflected forever because Mary's soul was a stainless mirror, and the whole soul of Jesus with His affectionate secrets and His sweet intimacies was always before her, united to her.

Mary's heart also reflected her Son's sacrifice of purity for the same causes and with the same fervent glow. In a certain sense it was the same immolation, although mitigated so that a mere creature might be able to withstand it.

And although Mary's immolation was less intense, it was longer in duration, for she endured it throughout the long years of her incomprehensible solitude without the sensible consolation of Jesus, without the support of her Son, feeling her desires and her grief mount up in the immensity of a desolate world.

Our Blessed Mother retraced all the stages of Jesus' immolation in the secret of her Heart. She experienced the expiation in the desert and the struggle with Satan; in spirit she accompanied Him in the public life, suffering because men did not understand her Son but offended Him ceaselessly with their baseness and ingratitude. The terrible conspiracy of the Synagogue against Our Lord shook Mary's soul with incredible grief, and when the hour of the powers of darkness struck, she gathered up in the Cenacle the testament of love and of bitterness from her Son's Heart, with Him she agonized in Gethsemane; and she participated intensely in all His sufferings and ignominies until the most sacred moment arrived when the sacrifice of purity was consummated. Then she occupied her maternal position at the foot of the Cross, as she had occupied it in the temple when she offered the holy Victim.

What a spectacle! Earth's supreme purity offering the Purity of heaven upon the immortal hill, both impelled by the same love, united in the same oblation, and burning with the same ardent desire of glorifying the Father and of saving the world. If we had penetrating eyes and sensitive hearts, we would never withdraw from that unparalleled, sublime, immortal scene before which all the paltry events of our history fade into insignificance.

As often as the sacrifice of Calvary is renewed upon the altar and within souls, that mystery of love and of purity is also renewed in an invisible manner, for in both Mass and martyrdom Mary's purity is always present, enveloping with its celestial mantle Jesus' purity, which is mystically immolated.

The Church does not forget Mary upon recalling the immolation of Jesus: she celebrates[5] the immolation of the Mother one week before the sacrifice of her Son and in the Sequence of the Mass for that solemnity she allows to overflow in inimitable stanzas all her love for Jesus, all her tenderness for Mary, all the loving desire of accompanying both in their holy immolations.[6] In the stirring ceremonies of those days, in the narrations of Jesus' Passion, ever ancient yet ever new, one perceives the sweet, stainless figure of Mary always near Jesus, discreetly veiled, but most delicately united to the holy Victim. In the three great days of the still greater week, the exquisite symbolism of the Church makes Mary shine in the midst of sorrow's darkness, as the only light that always shines when the others are extinguished, as the only hope that the world does not obscure, because it triumphs over suffering and death.[7]

Like Mary, souls ought to participate in the sacrifice of Jesus, as they ought to participate in His purity. Some will share with Jesus and Mary their interior sorrow, their redeeming sufferings, and they will expiate the iniquities of a corrupted world with the offering of their purity. Others will expiate at least their own offenses with repentance and penitential practices, with love and sorrow they will burnish the dust-stained purity of their souls. But all ought to live with purity, love and suffering in their days of health, in that acceptable time, so that by reflecting Jesus' purity, warmed by His love and carrying His blessed cross, they may be admitted to the paschal banquet, revested in the white robes of purity, having crossed triumphantly the Red Sea in which the old man perished and the new man rose with Christ, as the Church sings:

> The Lamb's high banquet we await
> In snow-white robes of royal state;
> And now, the Red Sea's Channel past,
> To Christ our Prince we sing at last.[8]

EASTER-TIDE

The Triumph of Purity

EASTER-TIDE

Chapter V

The Triumph of Purity

The Church possesses the secret of expressing joy as well as sorrow because her virgin soul is steeped in purity, and purity, as a reflection of God, holds all celestial secrets.

In my judgment, the Church is more admirable in her expression of joy than of sorrow. Who in this world of suffering does not know how to weep? But the formula of joy, — not the hollow, superficial happiness of worldlings, but deep, perfect joy, — only the Church knows that, and those who have received from her the ineffable inspiration of holy joy.

In the midst of the desolate night of Holy Week a cry of joy breaks forth in the liturgy of Holy Saturday, swift as a dart, too free to fit a human mold, immense and deep, like all that comes from heaven and struggles to return there. Amidst glorious chimes the hymn of Bethlehem resounds like a new canticle, with a more profound meaning, with more celestial accents; no longer does that immortal hymn express the simple joy of the manger, nor is it the happiness of hope ringing out a vague and distant gladness. It is the solid, overflowing joy of possession and of triumph; a joy victorious over suffering and death, a joy sure of itself, magnificent in its plenitude, rising to die no more.

As in all great human emotions and in all divine contacts, ordinary human language is inadequate for the Church to express her Easter gladness. But from her heart, ecstatic with jubilation, breaks forth a mystic word: *Alleluia!* Its mysterious syllables expand in the modulations of the sacred symbol as if to become eternal, as if to soar to the abode of perpetual bliss.

During the entire Resurrection octave, the Church seems not to come out of her unspeakable rapture; her joy seems not to recover its serene, human form until Low Sunday when the inimitable paschal hymns — especially the entire Vespers — reveal the Easter joy in a more earthly tone.

Throughout this celestial octave, the Church seems to sing the simple, — almost childlike — Sequence of the Mass as if she wanted to teach us that only the simplicity of pure souls can move at ease in the lofty regions of joy.

Paschal joy is the gladness of triumphant purity, the gladness of Jesus risen, which pours forth upon the world such an abundance of happiness that, as someone has said, "There should never again be sadness upon the earth after the Resurrection of the Lord."

What are our poor miseries and our superficial sorrows, even those that distress us most, compared with that immense reality of the definitive triumph of sinlessness over sin, of light over darkness, of love over hate?

The Passion was a combat, a gigantic duel between life and death, between sinlessness and sin. The Sequence sings of it thus:

Death and life
In a strange conflict strove,
The Prince of life who died,
Now lives and reigns.[1]

Life by dying seemed conquered, but death was defeated forever.

Jesus, divine purity, the whiteness of eternal light, impelled by an unutterable love, came to seek souls lying in the mire of sin. Only He could free them, only light can touch mire without being stained — only He is so pure that He can cover our wretchedness and destroy our sins with the splendor of His purity.

But it pleased Him to come as a mighty wrestler, as a grand conqueror, first in His own Heart and afterwards on Calvary. He engaged in the gigantic struggle between sinlessness and sin. What a terrific duel! The Heart of Jesus was broken by indescribable sufferings, His blood-stained body appeared as a cluster of grapes squeezed out in the winepress, upon the Cross were heaped up all ignominy and suffering; the power of darkness, in its transitory but terrible hour, threw all the forces of evil upon the Immortal Victim.

Satan seems to sing his victory over a lake of pain and of blood when Life dies, when Jesus inclines His head under the immense weight of man's injustice and of God's justice.

Was purity conquered, perhaps, in its generous effort to conquer sin? Our Lord's sad disciples, probably asked themselves this question when they saw the precious body of the Master disappear beneath the stone of the sepulcher, for their tear-filled eyes did not even faintly perceive the tremendous mystery.

But a woman whose heart beat with a fathomless, invincible love, returned from the sepulcher, radiant with jubilation, on the luminous Resurrection morning.

> What thou sawest, Mary, say,
> As thou wentest on the way.[2]

Simple souls ask the question in the charming Sequence.

> I saw the tomb wherein the living one had lain.
> I saw His glory as He rose again.[3]

From the depths of suffering and death, sinlessness arose victorious over sin to bestow upon the world the divine gift of joy.

Stupendous miracle of purity! It brought forth joy from the very heart of grief. The kingdom of joy will have no end, for Jesus did more than destroy sorrow; He transformed it into the throne, the fountain of perfect joy.

Across the centuries suffering will continue its triumphal march. Our Lord did not destroy it because He loved it, as one loves the victorious sword that slew his enemies. One would say that far from destroying suffering, Our Lord amplified and expanded it within human hearts, for since He lived upon this earth, souls realize the purifying power of suffering; sorrow is accepted more graciously, with deeper understanding. When Jesus touched suffering, He made it mighty because He made it divine.

But precisely by making it divine, Jesus made it the fountain of the purest and the most perfect joy; when He descended from the Cross, He left thereon sorrow and joy united and sanctified forever because He also left there purity and love.

Purity in reality is the perennial source of joy; God is unfailing joy because He is infinite Purity; heaven is complete joy because it is perfect purity.

When purity reigned upon this earth for those fleeting hours in the garden of delights in which God had placed man, it was impregnated with joy; but gladness fled from earth when the angel's flaming sword drove sin-stained man from paradise. The earth sprouted the thorns of malediction because purity went away to hide in heaven.

When infinite Purity descended from heaven and dressed itself in our flesh, true happiness returned to earth; when

Purity triumphed over suffering, coming forth victorious from the tomb, joy was scattered throughout the world like an exquisite, penetrating perfume.

Wherever there is a reflection of purity, there is a sparkle of joy; therefore children are naturally happy because they are naturally innocent, but when their glance fails to be transparent, the smile of joy disappears from their lips. Therefore the Scripture says that the heart of the just man is like an eternal banquet because his life is virtuous.

The joy that Jesus brought back to the world is not the happiness of either the earthly or the heavenly paradise because these are unacquainted with suffering and death; they stem from purity, which expands into love.

The joy that Jesus gave us was the gladness that arose from the tomb; it blossomed on the Cross; it was the exultation of His Resurrection lovingly communicated to us, as He had given us everything else that was His. He arose from the dead for us, just as He had been born for us, lived and died for us.

The thread of gold that joins purity and joy is no longer, as in the world's dawn, the sweet, serene love that moved gently beneath the virgin fronds of paradise, but the love covered with blood and ignominy struggling to the death with evil, the love that plunges into the ocean of sorrow to draw forth triumphantly the pearl of joy.

Easter gladness buds out of the heart of sorrow by a miracle of purity. It is the springtime of souls coming after sorrow's winter to fill them with light, color and perfume. It is like nature's springtime, which in these very days passes triumphant over the renewed earth. On the Lord's day everything is in flower, souls as well as fields:

> Behold, the happy days return,
> The days of joy for them that mourn;[4]

> For winter is now past, the rain is over and gone. The flowers have appeared in our land, the time of pruning is come; the voice of the turtle is heard in our land. The fig tree hath put forth her green figs; the vines in flower yield their sweet smell. Arise, my love, my beautiful one, and come.[5]

May souls who love the Victor listen to His sweet call; may those who have passed through the winter of sorrow, now washed in the Precious Blood, clad in purity's shining robe, experience the celestial springtime of joy.

The final word of the Christian life is not sorrow, but joy; however, in this world there is no joy without sorrow, and in no world is there joy without purity. Souls ought to live in a perpetual springtime because their spring is love and "neither death, nor life, nor angels, nor principalities, nor things present, nor things to come, nor powers, nor height, nor depth, nor any other creature"[6] can drive love out of our hearts. Neither anything nor anyone can tarnish the glory of that eternal spring nor dissipate its immortal fragrance.

Therefore the Psalmist invites us to serve the Lord with joy and the Apostle exhorts us to rejoice always in the Lord. Souls who have found the secret of purity and of sorrow have also found the secret of perfect joy; its perfect canticle is the Easter Alleluia.

That divine joy has never been so deep, so intense, so sweet in any soul as in the soul of Mary, Mother of Jesus. Magdalen was the first to announce the Easter gladness, but its rich first fruits were for the Blessed Virgin Mary whose possession of the deep sources of joy was unequalled by reason of her incomparable purity and her immense suffering.

Therefore the Church lovingly mingles Mary's name with the Easter Alleluia:

> O Queen of heaven, rejoice, alleluia,
> For He whom thou didst merit to bear, alleluia,
> Is risen as He said, alleluia!
> Pray for us to God, alleluia.[7]

Yes, most sweet Virgin, pray to the divine Conqueror for us who struggle amidst the darkness and the miseries of earth, so that we may find perfect joy; place deep in our souls the sources of joy; give us faultless purity and loving sorrow, so that from the very core of our being abundant torrents of joy may spring up while the moment draws near for us to immerse ourselves forever in the unfathomable ocean of joy!

ASCENSION, PENTECOST, CORPUS CHRISTI

The Effusion of Purity

ASCENSION, PENTECOST, CORPUS CHRISTI

Chapter VI

The Effusion of Purity

The month of May is rich in liturgical treasures, for its delicate, springlike charm is enhanced not only by dedication to Mary Immaculate, but ordinarily by the addition of the solemnities of Our Lord's Ascension, Pentecost and Corpus Christi.

An effort to designate those manifold treasures by a comprehensive, pious term is uncalled for, since all Christian feasts and mysteries have an amazing unity, the reflection of divine unity. But to continue viewing the liturgy under the aspect we have been contemplating, we shall call the aggregate of the liturgical mysteries of this month the *effusion of purity*.

The Ascension

Condition for the Effusion of Purity

Our Lord's Resurrection brought to the world the joy purchased on Calvary with suffering and death; but humanity received the precious fruits of the Cross on the day of Pentecost, because all the gifts that Jesus acquired with His sacrifice are derivations and effects of the first gift, the gift par excellence, the Holy Spirit, since the first gift of love is love itself.

But in order that the Holy Spirit might come and pour

Himself out "upon all flesh," it was necessary that Christ ascend into heaven, as He Himself taught us: "But I speak the truth to you; it is expedient for you that I depart. For if I do not go, the Advocate will not come to you; but if I go, I will send him to you."[1]

St. Paul lifts the veil of this mystery a little for us in his explanation of the priesthood of Christ. The high priest of the old Covenant, his hands stained with the victim's blood, entered the Holy of holies to pray for the people; thence the fruits of the sacrifice were bestowed upon Israel. Similarly, Jesus "entered once for all through the greater and more perfect tabernacle, . . . by virtue of His own blood, into the Holies, having obtained eternal redemption."[2]

Calvary, site of the divine Victim's sacrifice, recalls the tabernacle, of the old Covenant. The Eternal Priest, bearing on hands, feet and side the glorious, everlasting print of His Blood, must enter the true Holy of holies in highest heaven, so that seated at the right hand of the Father He might live always making intercession for us, and present us as the most excellent fruit of His sacrifice to the Holy Spirit, the inexhaustible source of all the gifts of God.

The divine, transcendent consummation of the sacrifice of the Cross was Our Savior's triumphant entrance into heaven; therefore when He ascended, He showered His gifts upon mankind through the Holy Spirit.

Holy Church commemorates and, in a certain sense, renews that mystery in the Canon of the Mass. The sacrifice is completed upon the altar, the miracle of the transubstantiation is accomplished, the Body and Blood of Christ are mystically separated under the species of bread and wine. The priest bows profoundly over the altar and prays to the Heavenly Father:

> "We most humbly beseech Thee, almighty God, command these things to be carried up by the hands of Thy holy angel to Thine altar on high, in the sight of Thy divine majesty, that as many of us who, by participation at this altar, shall receive the most sacred Body and Blood of Thy Son may be filled with every heavenly blessing and grace."[3]

The angel of whom the Canon speaks is, according to commentators, the Holy Spirit, to whom belongs all consummation. Upon introducing Jesus mystically immolated upon the altar into the divine presence, He renews, so to speak, the mystery of the Ascension. Then, a new Pentecost, or rather, the everlasting Pentecost, fruit of the eternal Sacrifice, fills souls with every grace and heavenly blessing.

The Ascension is, then, the divine complement of the Cross. When Christ Jesus ascended into heaven, He sent the Holy Spirit, whose effusion upon souls is the precious fruit of Jesus' sacrifice. The immolation completed to perfection, the effusion of Purity came upon this world.

PENTECOST
THE EFFUSION OF DIVINE PURITY

By His suffering Jesus not only acquired for us created purity, a reflection of eternal Purity, but He also gave us infinite Purity itself, the Holy Spirit, source of all purity. Jesus had promised to give us not only living waters but their very fountainhead. As He said to the Samaritan woman ". . . the water that I will give him shall become in him a fountain of water, springing up unto life everlasting."[4] On another occasion, He cried out to the multitudes: "He who believes in Me . . . from within him there shall flow rivers of living water."[5] The Evangelist adds: "He said this, however, of the Spirit whom they who believed in him were to receive; for the Spirit had not yet been given, since Jesus had not yet been glorified."[6]

Created purity cannot be granted unless uncreated purity is imparted at the same time. Purity is so noble, the grace of God is so excellent that it cannot be separated from God Himself, just as a rivulet needs to be connected with a spring in order to flow. Purity is divinization and nothing can be divinized if it is not united to the Divinity.

Jesus, who came to diffuse purity throughout the world, gave us His spirit. He gave the Sanctifier to us not only on the day of Pentecost; He is always giving Him to us, for the life of the Church is an interminable Pentecost. The external marvels, fruits of the extraordinary charisms that the Holy Spirit granted to the Apostles on Pentecost, are not wrought every day; but He continues pouring out the torrents of purity that He infused into their souls. The light, the love, the unction of the Holy Spirit course through the world ceaselessly, like a mighty river filling the City of God with joy.

In the beginning of time the Holy Spirit moved over the waters, and with His divine fecundity put order, harmony, light, life and beauty into chaos. In the same way He moves constantly over the world, renewing the face of the earth and pouring into souls of good will another light, another life, another beauty, all superior to those He strewed over the material world, because they are divine.

All purity, whether in the Church or in the individual soul, is attributable to the influence of the Holy Spirit. He is the Sanctifier.

> Without Thy Godhead nothing can
> Have any price or worth in man,
> Nothing can harmless be.[7]

To be pure is to possess the Holy Spirit; in the degree to which a soul possesses Him, in that degree it will be pure. This does not mean that souls may not possess created gifts of purity besides this Gift of the Most High, but that all these gifts come from the Holy Spirit, and those that have intimate connection with grace cannot remain in the soul if the divine Spirit does not dwell therein.

A comparison will help us to understand this doctrine. When the sun is shining, the earth is illuminated and warmed; it is full of life and happiness. The light, the heat, the energy imparted to things are not the sun, but they come from the sun, and they are so intimately connected with it that when the sun is hidden, the earth becomes dark and cold.

Thus it happens in souls. Grace and its cortege of gifts and virtues are not the Holy Spirit, but they are gifts that take their rise from that infinite Gift and are so intimately united with Him that, when the Holy Spirit departs from a soul, everything in it is darkness, cold, sadness, death.

Therefore the Church proclaims in the Pentecostal Preface that when Christ Our Lord sent down the Holy Spirit upon His adopted children, the whole world rejoiced with overflowing joy.

The purity, then, that Jesus acquired for us with His sacrifice is the Holy Spirit, infinite Purity and the only source of all created purity. The mystery of Pentecost, which is immortal in the Church, is the effusion of Purity.

THE EUCHARIST, EFFUSION OF THE PURITY OF JESUS

The most sacred Humanity of Jesus has intimate relations with purity. The effusion of the Holy Spirit is always the fruit of the Cross. Jesus' sacrifice on Calvary merited the glory of Pentecost, and the constant renewal of that sacrifice upon our altars maintains the perpetual Pentecost in the Church.

The most sacred Humanity of Jesus mediates in all the marvels of grace accomplished by the Holy Spirit, for theologians teach that the sacred Humanity is the instrument of all divine works in the supernatural order. Not only did Jesus merit all graces for us, but His Humanity is also the instrument in the divine production of these graces.

The source of purity in heaven is the Holy Spirit; on earth the source is the sacred Humanity of Jesus. He not only merited grace for us with His sacrifice, (that holy Humanity is not only the depository from whose plenitude we all receive) but He also influences its growth. That fountain of living water, draught for eternal life, proceeds from the bosom of God, but before being channeled into souls it forms wondrous cascades. It gushes into the Humanity of Jesus, of whose fullness we have all received, and, then before reaching us, it flows into Mary, Mediatrix of all graces, as we shall see later.

The Humanity of Jesus has remained with us in the Holy Eucharist; in that mystery of love Jesus accomplishes His unparalleled marvels in souls, and all operations of grace through the other sacraments are irradiations of that mystery, which in the Church, is the center not only of her worship, but of her life and sanctity.

The Holy Spirit and the Eucharist have divine connections; both mysteries are fountains of purity and of life, but not two separated fountains; united by an inexpressible harmony, they form but one and the same fountain.

Therefore, although the Sacrament of love was instituted

on the eve of the Passion, it was not dispensed in the Church until Pentecost. On that day the heavenly fountain, united with that of earth, would pour throughout the world the holy inundation of purity; when the Holy Spirit, the eternal Perfecter, would complete all that Jesus had established, which, like holy seeds, needed to be watered by power from on high in order to germinate.

The Church, having a profound sense of divine things, celebrates the feast of the Eucharist immediately after the solemnity of Pentecost, intertwining in the liturgy the mysteries that are intertwined in the designs of God.

Even in the Canon of the Mass, — masterly résumé of all mysteries because it includes their center, Jesus' sacrifice — the relations between the Holy Spirit and the Eucharist are ingeniously suggested. After the Consecration, the priest implores the Father to send the Holy Spirit to carry the Sacramental Jesus before the divine presence so that from those heights all graces and heavenly blessings may descend and at that moment fill those who have partaken of the Body and Blood of Jesus.

The Eucharist is the fountain of purity; souls and bodies are sanctified with the ineffable contact of the most holy Humanity of Jesus. Each Communion deposits in the soul and even in the body fertile germs of purity. The wisdom of God, who disposes all things with wonderful sweetness, desired that the divine reflection of purity, in order to reach our wretchedness, pass through the virginal Flesh and the precious Blood of Jesus, which are flesh of our flesh and blood of our blood.

By the ineffable contact of the Holy Eucharist even the mysterious seed of the resurrection is deposited in our lowly flesh. This, after all, is the perfection, as it were, of purity of the body because it is the plenitude of its divinization.

The Eucharist, the mystery through which Jesus spreads Himself out, so to speak, because He goes to all places and passes through all ages and enters all souls who wish to receive Him, is also an effusion of purity.

Someone has said that a single surge of either love or of suffering can save the world; the Holy Spirit and the Eucharist envelop the world in those two waves because the Holy Spirit and the Eucharist both come from Calvary and they extend upon the earth the empire of the Cross formed with love and suffering.

FROM MARY
PURITY IS DIFFUSED INTO SOULS

Before that divine surge reaches us, it passes through Mary; it is like a divine torrent leaping from the bosom of the Divinity into the Heart of Jesus and thence to the soul of Mary to be scattered throughout the flowery field of the Church.

The purity of the Holy Spirit is infinite Purity, that of Jesus is divine and human; the purity of Mary is human, but most perfect. Therefore, along this harmonious scale the ineffable gift of purity descends to us.

Mary is the masterpiece of purity wrought by the heavenly Father; everything in her is whiteness and beauty because she is the spotless mirror wherein God is reflected. Her name sounds forth purity, her image is white and luminous, her remembrance floods souls with something celestial, her love purifies gently.

Mary is the Mother of purity because she is the Mother of Jesus. She is the Mother of the Redeemer, and in the price of our redemption, that is, in the price of grace, her tears mingled with the Precious Blood; the divine suffering of the Son blends with the immense sorrow of the Mother. Whenever we receive Jesus, we receive something of Mary, for Jesus bears something of her in His most sacred Humanity. The Eucharist is the gift of Jesus, but in a certain way, it is also the gift of Mary.

Spouse of the Holy Spirit, associated as she was with the work of the Incarnation, Mary is also associated with all the marvels of grace, for they are all directed to the mystical reproduction of Jesus in souls. The Holy Spirit descended upon her on the day of Pentecost for the sake of the Apostles, and for the sake of souls He descends upon her unceasingly in the perpetual Pentecost of the Church.

The Holy Spirit is the fountain that produces purity, the Humanity of Jesus is its meritorious and instrumental cause; Mary is the most holy aqueduct through which the divine gift is distributed.

In order that souls be purified, it is necessary that the Holy Spirit be poured out upon them, that the Body and Blood of Christ nourish them and that Mary cover them with her virginal, maternal mantle. One would not understand the mystery of the effusion of purity if he did not understand the prerogative of Mary as Mediatrix of all graces.

May is the month of purity. Christian piety has dedicated it to Mary, no doubt, because it can bring to the Virgin's altar spring flowers from the pure hands of children; but also because it can bring to Mary the flowers of purity that the spiritual springtime — the Easter season and the solemnities of Pentecost and Corpus Christi — brings to bloom in our heart.

In the designs of God, nature and grace are intertwined; the divine mysteries, so rich in variety, are fused into a magnificent unity that we are slow to perceive. While heavenly light, warmth and fragrance rejoice our souls, earth's flowers perfume Mary's altars and form a carpet over which Jesus passes in solemn and jubilant procession.

But in these present days, our eyes do not behold that sacred Body; our hearts adore, and our hope promises us. . . .[8]

FEAST OF THE SACRED HEART

THE FOUNTAIN OF PURITY

FEAST OF THE SACRED HEART

Chapter VII

The Fountain of Purity

The entire month of June is fragrant with the divine aroma of the Sacred Heart of Jesus. Christian piety, with the clarity of faith and of love, has bound together the months of Mary and of Jesus, just as in nature the time of flowers is followed by the season of fruits. In the designs of God, Mary is ever the way to Jesus, the Root of Jesse from which rises the celestial flower upon which the Holy Spirit descends in His plenitude.

The sweet joys of May prepare for the intimacies of June. Where would the Mother lead souls devoted to her except to the Heart of her Son, ocean out of which rushed the torrents of grace that flooded her spotless soul and to which they must return, impelled by her maternal tenderness?

The purity of Mary, like all human purity, came out of the Heart of Jesus, and to that divine fountain it must return, drawing with it the souls purified by her virginal contact.

Marvellous unity of the works of God! Billows of purity from the bosom of God, stored in the Heart of Christ, poured out by Mary into souls, produce in them celestial flowers of virtue. That surge returns to the source from whence it came, retracing inversely the same stages; souls go to Mary, she introduces them into the Heart of Jesus, and through this divine Heart they reach the loving bosom of the Divinity.

Purity has two sources: one celestial, love; the other terrestrial, suffering. In the state of original justice, love would have sufficed to produce purity; but earth having stained us, God decreed that love and suffering unite to purify our souls. Love is of heaven; suffering, of earth; to produce purity it was necessary that love descend and suffering be exalted, that the dew of heaven be mixed with the tears of earth; that love, which of itself is joy, be changed into suffering, and that suffering, which of itself is punishment and wretchedness, be converted into praise and glory by being transformed into love.

Isaias sang the sublime mystery:

> Drop down dew, ye heavens, from above, and let the clouds rain the just: let the earth be opened, and bud forth a Savior; and let justice spring up together.[1]

Heaven gave love; earth, suffering; purity was born.

Long centuries prepared the masterpiece of supreme power, eternal justice and surpassing love. The Patriarchs rejoiced as they saw in the distant future the hope of the day of the Lord; the prophets predicted its advent trembling with respect and love; the types, following one another and intertwining like the golden links of a chain of love and of glory, caused not only words but even things themselves to be cries of desire and of hope. It seemed that love kept sweetly and slowly descending from Heaven while cleansing pain kept mounting up on earth to embrace eventually and to celebrate their eternal nuptials.

The Holy Spirit brought love from heaven, the Virgin Mary supplied the substance of suffering, and in the splendid abode of purity, love and suffering met each other, embraced, and blended the one with the other. "Mercy and truth have met each other: justice and peace have kissed."[2] Love transformed into mercy found suffering, — profound truth of our fallen lineage —, and when love and suffering united, God's justice and man's peace gave each other an ineffable, eternal kiss.

Then Jesus, fruit of heaven and of earth appeared, filled with love and with sorrow, so celestial that He is the Word of God and so terrestrial that He is the Son of man; so divine that in Him "are hidden all the treasures of wisdom and of knowledge,"[3] so human that tears glisten in His eyes and bitterness dwells in His soul. In Him, love, without ceasing to be infinite, descended even to the depths of suffering and death; in Him, suffering, without ceasing to be human, ascended even to the heights of the divine, since it was love, fecundity and purity. In Him "we saw and we touched the Word of Life"[4] that "while we acknowledge Him to be God seen by men, we may be drawn by Him to the love of things unseen"[5] and through Him "the substance of our frail human nature which He had taken to Himself was placed at the right hand of the Father."[6]

The Canticle says, ". . . he is all lovely."[7] His gentle, thoughtful, eyes, glowing with divine light; His lips, lilies that distil purest myrrh; His wondrous hands, filled with heavenly blessings; His sacred feet that leave the imprint of heaven wherever He walks; His words that are life; His miracles that are love; His smiles that are promises of beatitude. But more beautiful, more attractive and more desirable than all discernible by our senses is that which is hidden from our gaze: His Heart, formed of what is most exquisite in heaven and most stainless on earth, for the Holy Spirit placed therein all the love of heaven, and humanity gave all the love of earth.

In that burning furnace of love, in that unfathomable abyss of suffering, purity was fashioned by a divine alchemy, all the purity that is ever to be diffused throughout the world, for of that plenitude we all receive.

For thirty-three years that Heart carried its treasures hidden within it; but finally at the end of His life it broke with love and sorrow, its perfume escapes, and the whole world became imbued with its indescribable sweetness.

God willed to give our mortal eyes a glimpse of that mystery, through impressive symbolism. ". . . he who saw it has borne witness and his witness is true."[8] ". . . one of the soldiers opened His side with a lance, and immediately there came out blood and water."[9] The water and the blood that came out visibly from Jesus' Heart are symbolic of the torrents of purity that poured invisibly from the soul of Jesus, from His love and from His suffering. Jesus crucified provided the three elements, that, according to St. John, give testimony upon the earth: the spirit, the blood and the water — love, sacrifice and purity — and those three are one because they proceed from one single source, they form one single river of purity and they run into one single ocean of sanctity.

Slowly, with the divine and triumphant slowness of God, the Church, which during centuries from ". . . good treasures brings forth good things"[10] has kept on revealing to her children that hidden mystery. His Holiness Pius XI, in the Lessons of the new Office of the Sacred Heart of Jesus, shows us the liturgical development of the cult of the Sacred Heart until it reached its present peak, making the feast of the Sacred Heart of first class rank, with a new Mass and Office, precious jewels of liturgical piety.

The torrent of purity that broke forth from the divine Heart filled Mary's holy soul, making her the masterpiece of purity, the perfect, masterly work from which is to be showered upon all souls the divine inundation; for, although in our chronological order, Jesus is posterior to Mary and Calvary subsequent to the Immaculate Conception, in the divine logical sequence and in the order of eternity, Mary's purity is derived from Jesus' purity and the mystery of the Immaculate Conception is the mature fruit of the mystery of Calvary. The Church teaches that through the foreseen merits of Christ, God enriched Our Lady with grace and freed her from original sin and, consequently ". . . she was redeemed in a most sublime manner."[11]

From her and through her the purity that came forth from the divine Heart reaches our souls, "according to the measures of Christ's bestowal."[12] The liturgy of the feast of Mary Mediatrix of All Graces teaches us that it is the office of this Immaculate Virgin to distribute the torrential graces that gushed from Jesus' Heart, in these beautiful stanzas of the hymn at Matins:

O great flood of mercy, from crime us purging!
O unfailing ocean of graces divine!
Whence unending sevenfold stream bears to us
  Life and salvation.

Springs so sacred who shall dispense to mortals?
Task sublime to no one but Mary given,
She it is who this sacred wave doth pour out
  At her discretion.[13]

That stairway of light and of love along which purity descends to souls, serves also for souls, when cleansed, to ascend to the fountain of purity and of peace as the angels of God ascended and descended along the mysterious ladder of Jacob.

Souls go to Mary in search of purity, and the more pure they are, the more they feel the attraction of that Immaculate Virgin, that most pure Mother; they kneel at her feet, they rest in her lap, and they make their happy abode in her soul. Finding Jesus there, they are united with Him; through His Heart's wound they penetrate the Sanctuary of love and of suffering to be elevated to the bosom of God where all is consummated. There are three heavens, as it were, in which souls find love and happiness: the soul of Mary, the Heart of Jesus and the ocean of the Divinity.

The months of May and June with their devotional solemnities seem to mark the first two steps of that happy ascent. When May flowers fade away and the last hymns in honor of the Blessed Virgin die out with sweet melancholy, other flowers perfume souls and other hymns of love make them vibrant with gladness. Now, the solemnity of the feast of the Sacred Heart of Jesus invites souls to loving sacrifice as it shows them the treasury of that Heart both human and divine, glowing with flames of love, pierced by thorns, rent by a lance and crowned by the Cross.

TIME AFTER PENTECOST

The Consummation of Purity

TIME AFTER PENTECOST

Chapter VIII

THE CONSUMMATION OF PURITY

Imagine a turbulent river on its way to the ocean, flowing on a long, varied course, leaping over abrupt cliffs, gliding through flowery fields, plunging into deep channels, until finally near its goal, it broadens out calm and silent into a vast plain. Such is the liturgical life, ardent desire in Advent, innocent joy at Christmas, austerity in Lent, heavenly gladness at Easter and burning fire at Pentecost; during the long period after Pentecost it seems to expand in majesty and in silence.

The splendor of the great solemnities fades away with the feast of the Sacred Heart and with the feast of St. Peter and St. Paul. After the great variety of stages in the first half the liturgical year follows the apparent monotony of the "green" Sundays tinged with the melancholy of exile and impregnated with nostalgia for eternity.

It is not that the love nor the praise nor the divine enthusiasm of the Church has been exhausted, for its treasures, being divine, are inexhaustible; but that the liturgical life becomes deeper, more secret, more celestial in this final period of the year. Purified by suffering, illuminated by the light of Christ and anointed by the Holy Spirit, the soul feels already "drawn by him to the love of things unseen"[1] and its "citizenship is in heaven."[2] If it is enveloped in silence, it is because it has reached the region of the unutterable; if its exterior transports have become fewer, it is because it has found the one it loves,[3] in silence it enjoys the delights of union.

The liturgical year is a mystical reproduction of the life of Jesus and a type of the interior life of souls. After His Ascension, Jesus was hidden from the senses, but He revealed Himself to souls; when He finished His mortal life, His life in the Church, in the Eucharist and in the human heart became deeper and richer. In the same way, when a soul reaches the plateau of union, it finds the unspeakable calmness of the heights, a copy of heaven's peace.

The soul, who during Advent brightened up its own purity with the painful efforts of the purgative way, found in the lovable manger of Bethlehem the purity of Jesus; at the holy contact it passed through the stages of the illuminative way, guided by the "star that has no setting."[4] It saw that Light wax strong in the silence of Nazareth, consume itself in sacrifice on Calvary, flare up in triumph through the glorious Resurrection, ascend into heaven and inflame hearts through His Spirit. The splendors of that Light bathed the soul imparting a share in the divine mysteries; flooded with light and with love after the Pentecostal outpouring, the soul began the inexpressible, heavenly life of union.

The purity that was born in suffering and developed in light was perfected in love; the long, silent, rich period of time that comes after Pentecost is the consummation of Purity in the divine unity of love.

"A thing is perfect in proportion to its return to its beginning,"[5] said St. Thomas; and as the supreme principle of purity is the Divinity, purity is perfected when it is submerged in that infinite ocean of purity.

From that lofty height purity descended to our souls, passing through Jesus and Mary; to scale that divine height souls must traverse the same way that He, Heaven's gift, came to us but in an inverse sense, Mary most holy and even the Humanity of Jesus are but ways to reach the bosom of God, fountain of purity and its most blessed consummation.

The time after Pentecost is the longest part of the liturgical year because it is the symbol of heaven, which is eternal, and because it corresponds to the life of union that by essence is inamissible. The road is short, the fatherland is everlasting. Union is the reign of Jesus in souls and "of his kingdom there shall be no end,"[6] wherever it is established. Purity is immortal because it lacks the earthly germ of destruction and because it is the radiance of the Most High.

At the end of this period, which is the close of the liturgical year, one seems to be immersed in the mysterious eternal region; the feast of All Saints makes us feel the family ties that bind us with the blessed who, sure of their own salvation and yet solicitous for ours, wait for us and call us. All Souls' Day also turns our minds and hearts to the other life; and the Gospel of the last Sunday after Pentecost compels us to consider the mysterious passage of the centuries while giving us a glimpse of the dawn of the day without sunset.

This entire season is filled with the hope of heaven, with the desire of consummated union. The native land and the proper atmosphere of purity, is heaven; in this world purity feels like an exile and exclaims with the Psalmist "Woe is me that my sojourning is prolonged."[7] Like St. Paul, purity desires to be loosened from the final bonds that detain it here below in order to fly to the abode of whiteness and of light. Perhaps the liturgical color of this season symbolizes this hope and this desire, which are characteristic marks, according to St. Thomas Aquinas, of those perfect in love.[8]

The desire of heaven, which sometimes is converted into martyrdom, tinges the liturgical life of this period with a sweet, deep melancholy. This attitude on the other hand, is never really lacking in the life of the Church, even in the most jubilant solemnities, because it is impossible to approach God intimately without feeling homesick for heaven.

But beneath this delicate melancholy, souls who have arrived at union enjoy a profound peace more than in any other stage of the spiritual life. In the latter "the glory of the King's daughter is within,"[9] and one of the characteristics of that glory is "peace not as the world gives."[10] It is the peace of full light, satisfied love, secure hope; it is the peace of the soul who has quieted the voice of passion, who has established its spiritual sovereignty over its whole being, who has simplified its life in the rich unity of love; it is the peace of triumphant purity that passed through fire and water and now, free from the dross of the world, possesses itself in possessing God.

St. Augustine, most apt in epigram, defined peace as "the tranquility of order." Is not purity, perhaps, the true, deep order, and is not the consummation of purity the order made tranquil because it has reached its plenitude?

Before the superficial gaze that perceives only the sensible seeking splendor and noise, this liturgical period will be monotonous and lacking in interest; but for the intuition of souls that have the "perception of Christ," in the apparent monotony of this time the immeasurable wealth of victorious peace is hidden. The time after Pentecost has the silence of the sublime, the peace of the immense; it is silent as the firmament, tranquil as the bottom of the sea. All things upon reaching plenitude are enveloped in silence and mystery: science, developed in the wealth of research and in the majesty of argument, upon reaching the point, is resolved into a profound, simple glance; art, when it is genuine, is a secret, silent intuition; love, which sings along its thorny or flowery paths, is silent and hides itself when it accomplishes its ineffable mystery.

In its spiritual ascent, purity sometimes utters cries of sorrow and sometimes canticles of joy, struggle and triumph; it expresses its innermost affections in ostentatious, sensible manifestations; but when it has gained the summit it retreats within itself and is buried in the silence of its peace, or rather, upon ascending, it leaves the earth and begins to live in heaven. That new life, so rich and splendid, seems to us hidden and silent because neither symbols nor language of earth come near expressing it.

But in that celestial life there is perfect praise and the new canticle of which the Psalms speak; but what is a hymn for the heavenly Sion seems silence for us poor exiles; the feasts of eternity are a mystery for us who live in time.

The love that is the consummation of purity, the love that the Paraclete kindled when He poured Himself out into souls on the fiery Pentecost, now reaches its supreme and heavenly form, and hidden in the depth of souls, accomplishes its mystery and celebrates its feast, delightful but interior, rich but silent.

To live the ineffable life of this final period of the liturgical year souls need to be imbued with purity, anointed with silence, penetrated with that burning love that, according to St. Bernard, "burns sweetly," without great explosions, glaring flames and boisterous songs.

United to their God and enjoying interiorly the most sweet Beloved, souls live that heavenly life, scarcely touching the earth because "now they have their hearts fixed there where true joys are to be found"; and feeling the weight of exile and sighing for the eternal fatherland, in their innermost being the sweet melancholy of hope mingles with the unfathomable peace of perfect love.

FEASTS OF THE SAINTS

The Perfection of Purity

FEASTS OF THE SAINTS

Chapter IX

The Perfection of Purity

We have contemplated the divine mysteries of purity in the *Proper of the Season;* now, during these final days of the liturgical year, it will be pleasant and profitable for our piety to glean in the fertile fields of the *Proper of the Saints* the fruits of purity seen in these elect souls. We may learn from them how our souls ought to share in that divine life which the liturgy develops and symbolizes.

The souls of the saints are God's masterpieces, exquisite, celestial works of art. To contemplate them elevates the spirit to a high spiritual level where it forgets the prosaic spectacle of this world, burdened with miseries, sad and sometimes tragic. Divine purity with its other-world splendor, rich variety and indescribable harmony is reflected in the saints. Beholding them, we feel the loftiness of our origin, the glory of our destiny and the opulence of the true, eternal life which Jesus brought us and which should be our only life.

In the saints we discover to what a degree heavenly purity can absorb our frailty and transform our wretchedness, and through the magnificent example and efficacious intercession of those who are flesh of our flesh and bone of our bone, we feel impelled to open our souls completely to the divine inpouring and to allow the grace of God to accomplish in us its marvelous work.

August is the month of harvests: in our verdant orchards, tree branches bend earthward to the breaking point under the weight of fruitfulness, while innumerable butterflies and little birds flit about in the fragrant air. An admirable harmony intertwines the seasons of the year with the spiritual stages of the liturgical life, for the natural order is made to serve the supernatural. And so the saints' feasts celebrated during August make this month appear in the liturgy like a very prolific orchard bursting with fruits of sanctity and purity.

In the middle of the month, we observe with holy rejoicing the consummation of that purity which after Jesus' purity has never had anything similar to it, and which will never have an equal, Mary's purity, ineffably consummated in her glorious Assumption.

The imagination is lost and the mind confounded when we attempt to examine the firmament, to think about the innumerable stars strewn through it, the enormous distances that separate them, the fantastic peregrinations of stars that seem to travel through the infinite with incredible rapidity. But it would be easier for us to conceive of the immensity of the firmament than the immensity of Mary's glory, which exceeds our thought, surpasses our dreams, and which is lost in the inaccessible horizons of the supernatural world.

If it is now impossible for our smallness to appreciate the treasures of purity that the most holy Virgin received in the blessed moment of her Immaculate Conception, since those treasures surpass those of all the saints together, how could we estimate the augmentation of that purity in the long years of Mary's life, due to her perfect fidelity and the divine effusions that the sweet Virgin received in Nazareth, in Bethlehem, on Calvary and in the Cenacle? Virgin of virgins, Mother of God, inseparable companion of Jesus, Co-redemptrix of the human race, Mother of the Church, Mediatrix of all graces; all these titles accumulate incredible oceans of purity in Mary that even in heaven we shall but faintly perceive. Mary's perfect fidelity multiplied constantly, attracting new torrents with the irresistible force of her profound humility, stainless purity and perfect love.

If we cannot understand the prodigies that divine love accomplishes in the least of the elect, how can we guess what infinite love achieved in the most beautiful soul of all, the best beloved and the most intimately united to God, Mary's soul?

As teeming trees bend beneath the weight of their fruitfulness, Mary most holy died beneath the weight of her glory, under the splendor of divine light, under the inundation of celestial purity, under the fire of love "strong as death."[1] One day the immaculate body of Mary was no longer able to resist the ineffable effusions of the divine, and broken like a very delicate vase, it allowed the precious soul to escape, an exquisite perfume which the Beloved kept in His Heart. Meanwhile, the broken vase was repaired by Omnipotence and the mortality of the flesh was victoriously incorporated with immortality.

In the latter days of August, the exceptional purity of St. John the Baptist is consummated under the ax of an incestuous king. Sanctified in his mother's womb, grown up in the solitude of the desert, austere, silent, in intimate contact with Jesus, John accumulated in the days of his maturing youth treasures of virginal purity. When God's hour struck, the Voice of purity arose from the desert to resound in the corrupt world like the voice of an angel of God. His mission was one of purity; he did not come to communicate perfect purity to souls, but his baptism of water prepared them to receive the purity of the One who would baptize in the Holy Spirit. Humble even to heroism, virgin in the Old Law, most faithful Precursor of Jesus, his perfection was proclaimed by Truth itself. He crowned the purity of his life by dying for purity. Lust became cruelty in order to behead him, and, as has happened before and will continue happening, evil judged victorious when it kills the ministers of good, finds in its apparent, ephemeral victory its most profound humiliation, for it perfects the greatness of its enemies; it is converted into a bond servant and I would almost say into the best servant for the glory of the good.

The purity of the Apostles, like Jesus' purity, has two consummations, fecundity and martyrdom, which assuredly are united by a divine logic, for it is written that the grain must die in the ground before it becomes productive. All the Apostles suffered martyrdom to confirm with the supreme testimony of their blood the testimony of light and of love that resounded throughout the whole world in favor of Christ.

A form of purity, nourished with "sincerity and truth,"[2] is commemorated on August twenty-fourth, day of the martyrdom of St. Bartholomew, of whom Jesus said: "Behold a true Israelite in whom there is no guile."[3] Sincerity is that purity of soul that renders it capable of being filled with God's light, as the limpidness of the crystal disposes it to receive the sunlight.

After the Apostles, the martyrs show the ruddy fruits of heroic purity in the garden of the Church. They fill the liturgical year with their glory because they were innumerable in the first three centuries of Christianity and, thanks be to God, they never have been lacking and never will be lacking in the Church. Martyrs abound in the month of August. Among them two illustrious deacons are pre-eminent: St. Stephen, chosen for the sacred ministry through the merit of his chastity, a man whose countenance shone like that of an angel, "full of faith and of the Holy Spirit,"[4] the first to shed his noble blood for Jesus; and St. Lawrence who, after having placed in the hands of the poor the riches entrusted to him, went to his martyrdom serenely and joyfully, and even with the graciousness proper to his noble race.

Illustrious confessors illuminate the liturgy of August with their brilliancy. Consider St. Joachim, blest father of the ever Virgin Mary. The soul of the aged patriarch must have been a veritable abyss of purity, since from his fruitful stock came the incomparable purity of Mary. Next, St. Bernard, the contemplative, whose "conversation was in heaven,"[5] whose works bespeak celestial light and indescribable sweetness. When he speaks of Jesus and of Mary, his habitual serenity seems to be disturbed by a divine restlessness, by the burning enthusiasm of love. In him, purity appears particularly as light, — there is such a close relation between these two heavenly realities, — but it is light like sunlight, bringing warmth and life.

Another purity,—out of the mire,—shines in the month of August with the brilliance of genius and sanctity harmoniously blended in the mighty soul of Augustine. As the drop of dew, transparent and beautiful, leaves the earth that stained its purity and rises to the heights glittering wih sunlight, so the soul of Augustine, reformed by grace, was elevated to the heights of wisdom and of love, transported into the light of pure, serene regions.

In the final days of August, the gentle American maiden, St. Rose, scatters the fragrance of purity, a true rose cultivated with tenderness on the new continent by Jesus, the tireless Gardener. Its virginal fragrance contrasts strongly with the miasma of today's corruption! May her intercession preserve our faith safe and attain for us the true peace that only Jesus can give.

As the vision of heaven passes before the eyes of our faith in the liturgical cycle, the triumphal procession of the saints, clad in resplendent purity, with their celestial beauty, makes us forget the miseries of earth, and with their marvelous example they teach us the true life, which is *love, suffering and purity.*

Part Two

LIGHTS ON THE LITURGICAL CYCLE

THE ADVENT SEASON

KEY OF DAVID

THE ADVENT SEASON

Chapter I

Key of David

"O Key of David and Scepter of the house of Israel, who openest and no man shutteth, who shuttest and no man openeth; come and bring forth from his prison-house the captive that sitteth in darkness and in the shadows of death."[1]

The opening words of this antiphon, taken from Scripture, express the royal right and power of governing that belongs to Jesus Christ Our Lord as to no one else. To hand over the key signifies in the language of scripture "to bestow power." Christ Himself employed this symbol when He said to St. Peter: "And I will give thee the keys of the kingdom of Heaven."[2] Not only in the language of Scripture but everywhere the scepter is clearly the universal symbol of sovereign authority, of royal command. So then in this antiphon the Church invokes Jesus Christ as the one who possesses the fullness of royal power in the true House of Jacob, Holy Church, the Kingdom of God.

But let us note well that Our Lord's power of ruling and governing is not like that of earthly sovereigns. In the world this power looks only to the exterior; it is not something interior, profound, penetrating hearts. Authority in a nation, for example, is exercised upon external affairs; it watches over the rights and the duties of subjects so that the one may be respected and the other fulfilled for the maintenance of peace and exterior order. Jesus holds a different kind of power. It is interior and profound; it rules by dispensing life and happiness; its sweet yoke serves not only to establish exterior order in the Church, but also to bring order, peace, truth and love to the very depths of our souls. And so it is that Our Lord, by governing our souls, gives them life; by ruling them. He removes not only external obstacles, but also interior impediments; by exercising over us His sovereign power He penetrates even to the citadel of our hearts to purify and transform them.

The power of Christ has not only this character of inwardness and depth exclusively as its own, but it is also a power that is *absolute,* not relative; its action on souls bears the stamp of the definitive. Priests, whose powers are a participation of the sovereign power of Christ, can work not only on the exterior of souls, but also in their interior, by teaching them truth, infusing love, establishing order and peace. They can remove sin, purify, correct defects, teach the practice of virtue, and guide souls even to the summit of perfection. But this influence is not definitive. Priests hold the key of souls; they open and close; but when they close, another can come and open; therefore, their action on souls is very far from being conclusive.

How many times, for example, we priests, because we hold the key of David and the scepter of Israel, open the Kingdom of God to a soul, introducing it into the abode of grace, of light and of love; but the devil comes with his temptations, the world with its attractions, the passions with their rebellions, and they close it. To another soul we can open up new, broader horizons, horizons where life glows and happiness prevails; but in the lower regions of its nature rises a little cloud that gradually obscures that sky and closes those horizons. So it is that the action of the priest, though profound and intimate, is not final. We can open and close, but provisionally.

The power of Christ is not like this. It not only reaches even to the depths of souls but it is also decisive. What He opens, no one can close; what He closes, no one can open; for in His hands are life and death, happiness and affliction; for His word is most efficacious, it is omnipotent; His power is absolute and divine.

What happiness that He who possesses such power is coming to our hearts on Christmas! What He is coming to do in our souls will have this definitive character. If He opens to us the treasures of His grace, open they will remain; if He closes for us the doors of darkness and the shades of death, the splendid light of heaven will always shine in the firmament of our souls.

But some one might present this objection: how many times has Jesus opened for me the doors of life and happiness, and I, making bad use of that terrible privilege of liberty, have closed again what He had opened. Then how can His action be definitive?

It is undoubtedly true that we have the unfortunate prerogative of spoiling God's work and of distorting His divine designs; but we must also realize that we can resist God's plans, His most holy Will, in a very relative manner only. Sacred Scripture teaches us that no one can resist the will of God. The obstacles that our will places to it are not definitive. Jesus opens the door for us, we close it, but we close it in a provisional way. The only thing that He has to do to circumvent us is to retard His action a little; in place of following the direct, rapid route that He had proposed. He describes a curve, one of those beautiful curves that only God knows how to make. To prove this, let us see what Sacred Scripture teaches.

In the beginning of time, God opened to the human race the door of happiness, the door of original justice; it was a figure of that other celestial, eternal state of happiness with the very felicity of God. The devil came and closed the door by tempting our first parents to sin and thus they contaminated all human nature with their guilt.

But could the demon really close the door of happiness that God had opened? By no means; the only thing he accomplished was that the road to happiness was not that direct path, so easy, simple and delightful, which God had first selected. Centuries passed and then God described a wonderful curve, most wisely, lovingly planned: Christ died for us, and the door that God had opened at first, was opened again and remained open definitively. The devil could not close it except in a provisional manner; he could not frustrate the designs of God, he could only retard them. On the other hand, Jesus not only accomplished His plans, but accomplished them in a more admirable manner than had been originally conceived, as the Church observes in one of the prayers of the Mass: "O God, who in a wonderful manner didst create and ennoble human nature, and still more wonderfully hast renewed it . . ."

Is it not true that the curve of the Redemption is incomparably more beautiful, more profound, more exalted than the straight line of original justice?

On Pentecost Our Lord opened the door of the Church, the true House of Jacob. Souls by the thousands received the grace of baptism and through the ministry of the Apostles the Church began to be extended throughout the whole earth. But the demon aroused hatred against Jesus Christ and His work in the hearts of Nero, of Caligula, of Diocletian, and persecution came. Anyone might have thought that the door which Jesus had opened with the institution of the Church had been closed by the devil, placing a seemingly invincible barrier with the blood, torments and death of so many Christians.

But it was not so. The Church was not destined to be established by following a straight, secure and rapid route; for then the curve came, a curve of heroism and of glory, and three centuries later, upon the ruins of her enemies, the Church remained definitively established. The designs of God were accomplished in spite of the efforts of the devil. Far from closing the door that Christ had opened, the only thing the Evil One accomplished was to make it larger, wider, more glorious. Thus it always happens.

The same thing occurs in each soul. If we could only understand our own history! I think that the story of any soul is marvelous, even of those souls that some call common, (though I know not why, because I do not understand how divinely redeemed souls with a lofty destiny, who bear the seal of Christ's Blood and are nourished with the Holy Eucharist, can be regarded as common,) even those souls, I repeat, in whom everything seems ordinary, in whom nothing exceeds mediocrity according to our poor judgment; the history of even such souls is one of God's marvels.

If we could only realize what that most powerful King who holds in His hands the key of David and the scepter of the house of Jacob has wrought in our soul! How many times Our Lord opens the gate of life, and the devil or we ourselves instigated by the devil, close it! But what God opens, no one can close; what we do at the most is to retard God's plans a little, to make His designs trace a graceful curve instead of a straight line; for what He has opened for us, eventually will remain opened.

When Jesus loves a soul, when He sets His eyes and His Heart upon it, neither anyone nor anything, in heaven, on earth, or in hell is capable of tearing it away from Him. Each attempt to close love's door to the soul chosen by God only moves the Most High to carry out to the end a more admirable and beautiful masterpiece. Striking affirmations of this truth may be found in the history of the saints.

But it is not necessary to go so far away to find proofs. Let us enter the sanctuary of our own heart, there to review attentively our own story; we ourselves will be witnesses of this truth.

Since our Lord opened the door of His Heart to us, since He revealed to us His love and snatched us away from the vanities of the world, is it not true that all Satan's attempts and all our own resistance and ingratitude have not been sufficient to close the door that He opened?

Jesus has wonderful means for repairing His work. If we run away, He knows how to go in pursuit of our souls and to pierce them with His sweet voice so that we return to His arms. If we are too fond of some creature, Our Lord has means, sometimes very gentle, sometimes sharp and shocking, to detach our stubborn hearts. If we fall, He has at His service creative omnipotence to renew our soul and create in us a new man in justice and holiness.

How many times in moments of helplessness and pain, of calamity and misfortune, we have thought that all is lost forever! How many times we have recalled with bitterness the happy days when we loved Jesus and we are convinced that those graces will never return. Then we believe that the door of happiness opened to us by Jesus has been closed and will never again be opened.

Fortunately we deceive ourselves. What Jesus opens no one can close; what He closes no one can open. Let us hope! Let us wait! That bitterness of soul, that impotence oppressing our heart, — these are nothing more than the wonderful curve of the wisdom and the love of God who will accomplish His designs in spite of all obstacles, resistance and frailties. Is not this truly consoling?

Oh, if we might comprehend the meaning of those words of Scripture: "The gifts of God are without repentance," without retraction! When He has fastened His eyes and His Heart upon a soul, there is no creature in heaven, on earth or in hell that can drag it away from Him. Perhaps this is the meaning of those words of St. Paul: "For I am sure that neither death, nor life, nor angels, nor principalities, nor things present, nor things to come, nor powers, nor height, nor depth, nor any other creature will be able to separate us from the love of God, which is in Christ Jesus Our Lord."[3]

Ordinarily, these words are interpreted in the sense that the Apostle felt himself so firmly established in charity that he had the audacity to defy all creatures to pull him away from his love of God if they could. But I think that they can also have this other meaning: that the love of God for us is of such a nature, so firm and so deeply rooted in our soul that no one can take it away from us when God seals our soul with its definitive character.

Holy Church with her penetrating insight understands that power of Jesus so interior, deep and especially so final.

She cries out to Him, desiring that we join her in repeating the word proper to Advent,—the plea of the exile,—"Come!"

In heaven our song will express possession, felicity; from our lips and from our heart will break forth the "new canticle" of Holy Scripture. But in our banishment, although once in a while that heavenly chant flashes like lightning at midnight, ordinarily we can intone only the word of hope and desire: "Come! Come!"

This is the word of exile. Let us not tire of repeating it. If we lie in darkness and in the shadows of death, let us cry out to Him: "Come!" And He will come with His grace to purify us and to lift us up. If we sit in sadness and dejection, let us continue pleading: "Come! Come!" And He will come with His presence to scatter our sadness and with His help to strengthen our weakness. May the constant cry of hope and of desire never fail to rise from our heart; then each coming of Jesus will purify us, give us life, and make us happy by inflaming us with love.

Here on earth love has the strange prerogative of producing emptiness in our hearts the more it fills them; of producing a thirst the more it refreshes us; for each degree of love that our soul receives is a new desire for Jesus, a new vacancy hollowed out in it, a new degree of hope and of desire blossoming from the depth of our being. Hence, the more we love, the more we repeat the word of exile "Come!" Even when arrived at the peak of perfection, from that height we continue pleading, and with greater vehemence we utter the self-same word: "Come!"

Is it not this same word that forms the theme, so to speak, of the blessed symphony of this world while awaiting the consummation of time? At the end of the Apocalypse St. John paints with two masterly strokes — two phrases —

the history of the world since Jesus came twenty centuries ago until He will return to judge the living and the dead at the end of time: "The Spirit and the bride say 'Come!'; let him who hears say 'Come!' " . . . "Come, Lord Jesus."

Upon considering the fullness of the power of Jesus Christ and His firm, decisive action, the Church cries out to Him, but she does not limit herself to asking Him to come in a general manner as in the preceding anthems; she takes pleasure in explaining to Him our necessities, always using the language of Scripture: "Come and draw the captive out of his prison where he groans; come and free those who lie in the shades and shadows of death."

In these two figures are contained all our necessities; we are always captive, we are always lying in darkness. Without doubt we possess sanctifying grace, we have already left the lugubrious prison of mortal sin, mysteriously joined with the eternal prison of hell. Without doubt also, since grace has illuminated us we have left the shades and shadow of death, for now the light of life illumines us. But although we departed from that prison and although that light illumines us, is it not true that we still have not reached the fullness of that liberty which Christ brought to us? Consequently, it is necessary that Jesus come and grant us perfect liberty and illuminate us plentifully with His light so that the last vestiges of shade that still surround us may disappear.

Are not the disordered affections of our heart and the weakness of our will prisons keeping us captive? Are not the obstacles within ourselves to total surrender to Our Lord, to loving Him fully and definitively, bonds and chains holding us captive, hindering us from flying to our true and complete happiness? Are not the mistakes, the doubts, the vagaries of our reason and our conscience shadows and shades that obscure our way to God?

As long as we do not reach the heights of perfection we are captive, we carry darkness in our spirit, and therefore we ought to supplicate Jesus saying to Him: "Come and free the captive lying in the shades and the shadows of death."

When all the prisons have been opened for us and we have come forth free, when all the shadows on our spirit have been scattered; still the prison of exile remains for us, still we shall sigh for the supreme liberty of heaven.

All of us, then, just and sinners, imperfect and saints, ought to cry out to Jesus and say to Him with our whole heart and soul, with the ardor and the vehemence with which the Church says it: "O Key of David and Scepter of the House of Jacob, come and free the captive who lies in the shades and shadows of death!"

And we shall say to Him in more simple, intimate and familiar speech: "O Jesus, open to us forever the doors of Thy Heart! For if we enter that divine Heart, we shall leave in the distance the shades of sin and of the world; if we enter that ark of peace, all our chains will fall, broken into pieces. O Jesus, Thou who openest and no one can close, open to me light, love, happiness and life forever!"

THE CHRISTMAS SEASON

The Mystery of Weakness

THE CHRISTMAS SEASON

Chapter II

The Mystery of Weakness

In the long centuries that preceded the coming of Jesus, the Prophets seeing Him in the mysterious distance painted their magnificent vision with vivid colors. All the wealth of the oriental imagination was requisitioned to reveal the glorious theophany.

His name is Wonderful, the Strong, the Omnipotent; He bears an empire upon His shoulders. His glory will cover the heavens and His praise will fill the earth. His brilliance will be as the light, in His hands He will carry resplendent rays, there His strength will be concealed. He will look at the earth and nations will be dissolved, age-old mountains will crumble, and hills will be bent when He spreads over them the eternal roads. The mountains will see Him and will be moved, the abyss will cry out, and the deep will declare His power. In His presence the sun and the moon will stand still; then they will move in the light of His arrows, in the splendor of His flashing spear. He will rise up in the midst of the people as a standard; before Him kings will be silent and nations will send Him their supplications.

But, what a striking contrast between prophecy and history, between figure and reality!

The event predicted for so many centuries was verified finally in an unknown corner of the earth, at midnight, in the midst of universal silence.

Some shepherds watching their sheep were the first to be acquainted with the prodigy; the angel of the Lord announced to them the good tidings, and so that they might succeed in discovering the marvel, he gave them as a sign, not the glories that the prophets had foretold, but these features disconcerting in their strange simplicity: "You will find an infant wrapped in swaddling clothes and lying in a manger."[1]

An infant . . . wrapped in swaddling clothes . . . lying in a manger! All weaknesses and all miseries are here; those of man that are many, those of infancy that are greater, and all aggravated by the burden of an incomprehensible poverty and abandonment.

Is this the One whom the Prophets had foretold? Here is a mystery, a mystery not restricted to Bethlehem, but one to be found as the nucleus of all Christian mysteries: *the mystery of weakness*. Every page of Scripture speaks to us of that mystifying weakness, all Jesus' mysteries bear it like a seal.

The strong man armed was in possession of the earth covered with shadows and with malediction; poor humanity agonized among the formidable temptations of Satan's gloomy tyranny. How will the world be saved? How will the Lord redeem a chosen humanity? Will he rise up as the powerful one inflamed by wine, of whom the Scripture speaks, to pursue his enemies and destroy them? Will he stand up, magnificent and terrible in his strength, to break the power of hell, as one breaks the fragile vase of the potter?

No, in order to destroy the formidable dominion of the devil, the *Omnipotent One will become small, He will humble Himself.* Listen to the word of the Evangelist: "And the Word was made flesh."[2] Listen to the commentary of the Apostle: "He emptied Himself."[3]

He will pass through the world doing good, pouring out light and life; but His passage will not be the triumphal march of power, but the silent pilgrimage of weakness.

As a child, a tyrant pursued Him; but in order to elude those deadly snares He did not have recourse to a miracle—God's weapon, nor did He employ shrewdness or power—the weapons of the strong, but He had recourse to flight—the resource of the weak. In the middle of the night Joseph took the Child and the Mother to the strange land of Egypt.

As a youth He buried Himself in the silence of Nazareth; He did not speak, He produced no masterpiece, nobody knew Him; His life was common, ordinary, almost vulgar. What are thirty years of the life of God upon earth? *A mystery of weakness!* But the shades of that silence will be scattered; one day the Light of the world will shine brilliantly. Jesus will leave Nazareth to sow His words of life, to astonish the world with His heavenly prodigies; to inflame hearts with divine fire; then we shall see Him as the Prophets saw Him, magnificent, terrible, adorable in His holiness.

Yes, He will come out of Nazareth, and He will push into the desert seeking another deeper weakness, that of penitence; He will crown the humiliating forty-day fast with the opprobrium of temptation, the frailty that comes closest to sin, the one that places Jesus in contact with the Accursed.

During His public life, Jesus will speak as no one has ever spoken upon this earth; but the strength of His word is His weakness. He does not use the resources of learning nor the artifices of eloquence; "in the persuasive words of human wisdom," according to the expression of St. Paul: the charm, the vigor, the divine efficacy of His speech is in its disconcerting simplicity, in its extreme unpretentiousness.

His miracles, at least His miracles, will reveal the Omnipotent. Who but God can command the wind and the waves? Who but He can tear away its prey from death? Yet, upon the divinity of His miracles Jesus will place the seal of weakness.

With mud and spittle He will make the blind see; He will veil the power in Lazarus' resurrection with the weakness of loving tears.

Even on radiant Thabor He speaks of His Passion; even on His body so magnificently glorified by His resurrection, He preserves the eternal, blessed mystery of weakness in the most sacred wounds.

But this mystery reaches a divine extreme beyond the power of human language to express in the sacred Passion. Gethsemani! . . . The Praetorium! . . . Calvary! . . . Let us adore in silence the culmination of the mystery.

Jesus Christ, who is of yesterday, today, and of all ages, lives in His Church and especially in His Eucharist an ineffable life which exemplifies the mystery of helplessness.

Indeed, the Eucharist seems made to preserve, to crystalize the weakness of Jesus! It is the compendium of them all; there are the smallness and the poverty of the manger, the silence of Nazareth, the blessed simplicity of the public life and even the accursed contact of temptation in the interminable sacrileges. The Passion is there, not in figure nor in remembrance, but the living, palpitating, true Passion. To the weaknesses of the life and death of Jesus, the

Eucharist adds another unbounded helplessness peculiarly its own. Yes, the Eucharist is the mystery of weakness!

> God only on the Cross lay hid from view;
> But here lies hid at once the manhood, too.[4]

On the cross the splendor of the divinity was hidden, but there remained the majesty of man, the glory of martyrdom. On the cross Christ spoke, spoke as always words of eternal life; the cross was His throne, from it He dispensed mercy, life and love, and even in the last moment, as He accepted the languor of death, the earth trembled and the sky was covered with darkness.

In the Eucharist Jesus does not speak, in the Eucharist Jesus does not work, and if the wicked place their sacrilegious hand upon Him, the earth does not tremble nor is the sky darkened. *The Eucharist is the last word in weakness.*

The life of the Church is the prolongation of the astounding weakness of Christ in the world. For twenty centuries the Church has been a spectacle of weakness upon the earth, or rather, the compendium of all human weaknesses.

Everything has contributed to this condition: Caesars and barbarians, heretics and scholars, kings and people; she has been persecuted in the name of science, in the name of power, in the name of liberty, in the name of equality, in the name of everything.

The Church has every weakness; while the latest of the dreamers endeavor to base their scientific theories on an idol of demonstration, the Church makes not the least pretense to demonstrate the revealed truths that she teaches, truths that she explains without ornament or artifice; those truths are undemonstrable on earth. The Church does not resort to political schemes nor to force of arms, nor will she ever do so.

Instead of the diplomatic flexibility that would solve innumerable conflicts, the Church possesses the holy intransigency of truth and justice, and she would prefer to stain the entire earth with her blood than to comply with the base demands of a tyrant.

How often her friends say to her: "You have the right and the prestige and the number and the authority. Say one word to your children, and with victorious sword, they will destroy your enemies and place you upon the throne of the world." And, like her divine Master, she will answer gently: "You know not of what spirit you are. My weakness is my strength; it is precisely because I do not have what the world calls strength and power that I am great, that I am immortal."

O Church of God, ever persecuted and ever victorious, your ineffable life is a mystery of weakness!

But it is singularly interesting to consider this mystery in the life of souls, another aspect of the mystical life of Jesus.

Wherever Christ is born, whether in a heart, a home or a village, the scene of Bethlehem is re-enacted. The angel of the Lord announces joy: "I announce a great joy," and he adds: "This will be the sign to recognize it: you will find a child wrapped in swaddling clothes and lying in a manger." The signs of Jesus are always the same. Seek the place where smallness and weakness are found; there is Bethlehem, there Jesus is hidden.

The conversion of a soul for Christ is a mystery of weakness. In order to be converted souls need to be thrown down like Paul on the way to Damascus; the soul finds Jesus when lying in the dust trembling with amazement.

Furthermore, the enigma of powerlessness is present in all stages of the Christian life. God pours His graces only in the cavity that holy weakness hollows out in hearts; God elevates only those souls who are deeply conscious of their misery; and when it pleases Him to raise them to the heights of sanctity, He lowers them first into chasms of oblivion unsuspected by the human heart.

The strength of the human heart lies in weakness. St. Paul, who possessed the secret of concise, energetic expression, condensed the mystery of weakness into this untranslatable formula: *"Cum infirmor tunc potens sum."*[5]

Oh, if souls only understood the doctrine of weakness! If self-love did not hinder them from esteeming the high value of their own wretchedness!

In the eyes of men we may be valued for our talent, our character, success in our undertakings; in the eyes of God, our worth may be measured by the weight of our wretchedness, of those miseries that the love of God leaves with us and that the love of our hearts accepts with resignation.

Neither the success of our efforts, nor the fruitfulness of our works can glorify us; but we can, indeed, glory in our wretchedness, as the Apostle did, so that the strength, the power of Christ may dwell in us. "Gladly, therefore, I will glory in my infirmities, that the strength of Christ may dwell in me."[6]

What can those infirmities be? What attraction can they have for the Heart of God? What efficacy can they have for transforming our hearts?

O souls who groan under the weight of your frailty, souls who feel yourselves far from God, enveloped in the suffocating atmosphere of your helplessness, do not forget that the signs for discovering Jesus are not the glories of Thabor but the simplicity of Bethlehem. Do not seek Jesus in the splendor of honor nor in the sweetness of consolation; seek Him in the dregs of your own destitution, in the poor, narrow manger of your own impotence.

Do not fear that your deficiencies may border on the cursed limits of sin. Look: on the high sea, travelers contemplate in the distance the ocean touching the sky; it seems a slender line on the far-away horizon; but that line is the immense distance that separates the earth from the sky. How many times our anguished souls look with fright into their secret conscience at the fine line that joins desolation with sin, without understanding that this line signifies the *infinite distance* which separates temptation from consent, desolation from sin, earth from heaven.

Even on the peak of perfection the problem of human weakness exists. The saints, as no one else, possess strength: strength to love, to suffer, to attempt anything for God and man. And why would they not have their human limitations? The world considers them especially weak. "In the sight of the unwise they seemed to die . . . but they are in peace."[7] They seem dead to the fools who see in them only the cross, the symbol of all weaknesses; but in reality the saints live in peace, the supreme strength.

God leaves them human failings so that in the midst of their unworldly life, their blessed victory, the undiscerning may reproach them with the words once spoken to Roman conquerors: "Thou art human." Then the ineffable magnitude of their graces will not exalt them, just as the mystifying "sting of the flesh" served St. Paul as a counterpoise to the stupendous revelations vouchsafed him. God left to the saints humbling traits so that He might be glorified, as an artist sometimes leaves on his masterpiece evidences of the coarse cloth transformed by his genius.

Still more, although the saints may not have shown external miseries, doubtless, they did suffer interiorly from their human limitations, which seemed so great to their God-enlightened minds.

And, as if their own wretchedness were not a sufficient basis for their extraordinary strength, God placed in them the miseries of others, as He placed all our deficiencies on Jesus.

However high a soul may be elevated, it fortunately never loses its infirmities; or rather, the more it is elevated, the more evident is the mystery of powerlessness within it, that weakness, which in this world, constitutes its strength.

And why do I say in this world? I suspect that even in heaven something of that strange mystery remains. The wounds of Jesus in His glorified body, the Lamb that St. John saw slain, as it were, make me think that in heaven *glorified weakness* will be preserved, as in the promised land the manna of the desert was kept in the sacred ark for a sweet remembrance.

THE LENTEN SEASON

Sorrow and Joy

THE LENTEN SEASON

Chapter III

Sorrow and Joy

The sacred liturgy presents two exhibitions of heavenly joy: the one of the Christmas season and the other of Eastertide. The first is ingenuous and sweet like the smile of a child; the second, deep and solemn as a replica of heaven. In the first, angels intone the canticle of hope; in the second, men have learned the eternal canticle, the mysterious *alleluia* of the blessed. The first breaks forth from an unforgettable manger; the second, from a glorious sepulcher. The first is the joy of springtime teeming with perfumes and hopes; the second is that of autumn laden with rich harvest. The joy of Bethlehem is the gladness of earth presaging heavenly bliss, while that of the Resurrection is the joy of a new possession and triumph.

During Lent and Passiontide these two outbursts of joy are bound together by a ring of austerity and sorrow. Even in the spiritual order that law of human life described in Scripture is fulfilled: "Laughter is mingled with sorrow and mourning fills the confines of joy."[1]

We should like that it were not so; like Peter, we would wish never to come down from Thabor, we would desire that the final notes of Bethlehem's song blend with the accents of the Easter alleluia.

We know not what we want, as Peter knew not what he said on the night of the Transfiguration. No doubt the joy of Bethlehem was necessary, that joy not formulated by human lips but sung by the angels of God. That happiness was necessary to open our hearts to hope, to teach us that God lives with us, to let our mortal eyes see the salvation of the Lord.

But to have joy come from our own heart and soul, to know the secret of happiness and to learn the canticle which expresses it, we need to experience the suffering that cleanses and strengthens, elevates and transforms, and still more, the suffering that redeems and blots out with divine Blood the sins of the world. The paschal alleluia is the precious fruit of two sorrows, divine sorrow and human sorrow sanctified.

Before the Church designed with such delicacy her marvellous liturgical cycle, Jesus outlined it in a living manner when He walked upon the earth. What was the life of Jesus but two divine joys united by a circlet of indescribable sorrow? The song of Bethlehem faded away in a gentle cadence in the silence of Nazareth, and one sacred night the triumphant hymn of undying joy burst forth from the glorious sepulcher; but between the two canticles, the first, sweet and simple as an idyll; the second, heroic and sublime as an epic of glory, are the austerity of the desert, the hardships of the public life and the unspeakable sufferings of Gethsemane and of Calvary.

The apostles did not comprehend the divine reason for that strange relationship, as neither do we understand until the light of God illuminates us.

> "From that time Jesus began to show His disciples that He must go to Jerusalem and suffer many things

> from the elders and Scribes and chief priests, and be put to death, and on the third day rise again. And Peter taking him aside, began to chide him, saying, 'Far be it from Thee O Lord; this will never happen to Thee.' He turned and said to Peter, 'Get behind me, Satan, thou art a scandal to me; for thou dost not mind the things of God, but those of men.' "[2]

In the narrowness of human judgment there is no room for the majesty of suffering; to understand it one must meditate on the divine, experience the divine, and relish divine things. Without Calvary there would be no Resurrection; without the cross there would be no "perfect joy" in this world.

The joy of Bethlehem is not perfect joy; the star of the Magi, however radiant it may have been, disappeared into the depths of the firmament; the song of the angels was something heavenly but ephemeral, like those waves of distant harmony that the fleeting, changing winds bring to our ears. Perfect joy is that which has its abode in the inner sanctuary of the soul; and the soul does not possess the secret of supernatural happiness until suffering transforms it; nor do lips know how to sing the canticle of heaven until they have been tempered by the bitterness of sorrow. To sing one must have wept; to feel the joy of heaven one must have travelled the rough, bloody paths of earth.

In their interior lives, souls need to travel a cycle of joy and of sorrow, like Jesus, like the Church.

Who has not felt in his heart the joyousness of Christmas? One day the soul perceived that something other-worldly had broken the monotony of her life embellishing it as the earth is beautified at dawn when the sun pours upon it the gold of its rays. An angel or a star was the herald of joy, and in the manger of her nothingness, covered with the straw of her wretchedness, the soul divined, rather than saw, the charming Babe who captivates hearts.

The jubilation of the Nativity is unforgettable; it has an incomparable charm. Later on, the soul will receive clearer lights and deeper joys; but that brightness of dawn, that fragrance of springtime, that youthful fascination of the first contact with Jesus, the first word of love, the first tender emotions, the soul will never experience again nor can she ever forget them.

The ingenuous soul thinks that this joy will never pass away. She will know how to guard the divine treasure; she will love Jesus so much and in such a way that it will be impossible for Him to depart. Upon her knees, transfigured with bliss she will live adoring, loving, lulling the Child of her heart and she will bind Him to her forever with the soft but unbreakable chains of love.

One day, nevertheless, gladness takes flight from the soul like a pleasing, passing dream. Could she have been unfaithful to love? Would Jesus have become tired as we often tire of what we love? No longer are the angelic hymns heard, no longer does the mysterious star shine in the sky and especially, no longer does Jesus fill the manger of the soul with His unique beauty, with His incomparable Sweetness. All around the soul is silence; but not the silence of Nazareth eloquent with love, but the silence of the desert, desolate and immense, and in place of the charming Babe the demon is nearby with his polished cunning, his cruel irony, his malignant influence, inviting the soul to sit down at the banquet of life, to ascend the pinnacle of pride as he displays before her astonished eyes the brilliant spectacle of the glory of the world.

Bitter struggles ensue, night without stars, solitude without comfort, a deep abyss in which everything, even hope, seems buried.

What has happened? The fact is that Jesus must suffer in chosen souls. There He must be delivered into the hands of His enemies just as in His mortal life, and there they must scourge Him and crucify Him so that He may rise on the third day. For He always does rise on the third day; although the hours of those days may seem centuries to the suffering soul.

In vain do souls think when suffering and the cross are predicted that their own path is smooth and strewn with flowers; in vain do they say like Peter—immortal type of the human heart that wishing to live on Thabor is scandalized by Calvary—"Far be from me, Lord, what You foretell. In truth can such suffering be mine?" Jesus in His love for souls, takes them to the desert, to the struggle, to martyrdom, so that they may learn to relish divine things after their taste has been saturated with bitterness, and so that from the dregs of sorrow perfect joy may evolve, a joy whose star has no setting and whose song is immortal.

Blessed the souls who after struggle and sorrow find Jesus, as did Mary Magdalen near the empty sepulcher, in the midst of the fragrance of a garden in spring! He is the same Jesus of Bethlehem, He who revealed His tenderness to them in the happy, bygone days, He who hid Himself in days of trial so that they could suffer. But being the same,

He now seems more beautiful, more loving, more their very own to the souls who find Him again after the night of the Passion, after the dusk of Calvary.

And in the midst of the blooming garden, like a divine outburst of perfect joy, two words are heard, deep and sweet, a whole poem of love: "Mary!" . . . "Master!"

I think that Jesus travels the mysterious cycle in communities as well as in individuals, for the spiritual life of a people, if it may be so called, is also a night of struggle and of suffering between two divine dawnings of joy; it is fitting that in nations, too, Christ die and rise again on the third day.

But men are always scandalized at the cross because they do not have the sense of divine things; they are familiar with human triumphs in which the conqueror, in a halo of glory, gloats proudly over the corpses of his enemies and the ruins of a fortress taken by blood and fire. Twenty centuries have not sufficed for man to understand the triumph of Jesus, to know that He always conquers in this way: His face spat upon, His flesh scourged and nailed to the Cross.

Four centuries ago we had our jubilant Nativity; we found Jesus, not guided by the light of a star, not led by the angels of God, but we found Him in Mary's sweet embrace.[3]

The canticle of Bethlehem was prolonged in the silence of the colonial centuries; afterwards came the austerity of the desert, the hardships of the public life and the suffering and ignominy of the Passion.[4]

But here as everywhere, Jesus will rise on the third day, and then we shall intone the *alleluia* of perfect joy.

In which watch of the night are we now? How many hours until the purple of the dawn tinges the east of our sky?

We do not know the future, nor do we need to know it, for in order to console us in our affliction and to nourish our hope one word suffices, that word in the Gospel filled with divine strength and heavenly sweetness, which emanates from the Heart of Jesus: "Confidite!," "Have confidence, I have overcome the world!"[5]

THE EASTER SEASON

Perfect Joy

THE EASTER SEASON

Chapter IV

Perfect Joy

Perfect joy, according to St. Francis of Assisi, consists in the "suffering of many things for the blessed Christ who desired so greatly to suffer for us." At first sight it seems strange that joy consists in suffering; but if one delves into the mysteries of joy and of sorrow, he discovers that these two seemingly opposites are intertwined in the deep mystery of love.

Joy springs from satisfied love, and pure, perfect love finds complete satisfaction in suffering for the beloved, because love is the gift of self, and upon earth the fullness of that gift is realized in suffering.

This explains the passion of the saints for pain and sorrow and the exquisite joy they experienced when suffering.

Herein, especially, lies the key to that inexpressible joy which Jesus must have felt in His innermost soul while enduring all His torments for the glory of the Father and the good of souls.

His sorrow was as immense as His joy, and these two immensities, established upon love, dwelt together in Jesus' Heart, but with each one preserving its own proper character through the marvellous efficacy of that same love.

Nevertheless, I dare to think that St. Francis of Assisi in his charming parable expressed only one of the forms of perfect joy and that in this sad exile there are other emanations from Paradise which merit the name of perfect joy.

Perfect joy is, in very truth, the fruit of perfect love; joy is the fragrance of that celestial flower of love, the splendor of that living flame, the sweet resonance of that divine harmony. When love becomes despoiled of all egoism, when its essence shines with royal purity, when its victorious activity reaches the plenitude of its expansion, when it fulfills completely its blessed mission, then the perfume becomes exquisite; the splendor, glorious; the resonance, sublime; then love produces, like a heavenly fruit, perfect joy.

But in order to understand this matter it is necessary to plumb the very nature of love.

On the part of the lover love is a giving; to love is to give oneself, it is to make the oblation of one's whole being. Therefore, God is love,[1] because His life consists in infinite givings in an ineffable, divine way.

We creatures are capable of loving in the degree in which we are capable of giving ourselves. The supreme gift of man in the present state is the offering of pain and of death. Therefore, Jesus said that "No man has greater love than he who gives his life for his friend."

Perfect love on earth is that which reaches the heroism of suffering and of death. This love produces the miracle of perfect joy.

Viewed in relation to the Beloved, love consists in desiring the good for him.

Philosophers say that all things desire good, but in this love which we are considering, it is not his own good that the lover craves; love has changed the center of his heart, has transformed his soul's desire, making him come out of himself, to project his powers outward; the lover seeks the well-being of the Beloved as the only good, because that good is his own good.

Who will understand what is contained in this very simple formula: To love is to desire good for the Beloved; to take complacency in the good that the Beloved possesses; to want for him what he does not have; to toil, to suffer, to die if necessary, for the welfare of the Beloved? All this is to love.

Since the supreme good of all beings is happiness, perfect love delights in the bliss of the Beloved, forgetful of his own; it is the lover's desire to make the Beloved happy, and when this is attained, the lover's happiness is complete.

To take pleasure in the happiness of the Beloved is perfect joy, because it is the fruit of perfect love.

The perfect, the supreme joy of the Blessed Trinity consists in taking infinite complacency in its eternal, inexhaustible, incomprehensible beautitude.

To take complacency in the happiness of God was also the perfect joy of Jesus' soul; this is the joy of the blessed, and souls that attain perfect love in this life participate therein. Without doubt this was the joy of which St. John the Baptist spoke to his disciples: "He who has the bride is the bridegroom; but the friend of the bridegroom who stands and listens rejoices on account of the voice of the spouse. Thus is my joy fulfilled."[2]

Easter gladness corresponds to this form of perfect joy. We rejoice because Jesus rose from the dead, because having risen, He achieved every victory, because with Christ's resurrection the glory of God has shown plenteously upon the earth. The *alleluia* encloses within its mysterious syllables the happiness of praising God. It is a canticle of perfect joy.

But there is a secret delight in the fact that the happiness of the beloved may be the gift of our love. Thus, God takes immeasurable satisfaction in making souls eternally happy. What must be Jesus' delight in having secured that happiness with His own Blood! Who will say that this is not perfect joy?

We can participate in that divine joy. We cannot give God essential good but we can give Him accidental good, that is, glory. After God Himself there is nothing so great as His glory, and if rightly understood, the glory of God is the only greatness and the only good, since the happiness of creatures is nothing else than the reflection in them of the glory of God.

So great is the glory of God that it is the supreme end of all God's works in the natural order as well as in the supernatural. Jesus sought nothing else, as He Himself testified: "I honor My Father. I seek not my own glory."[3] When He thought about the glory of His Father, He rejoiced in the Holy Spirit,[4] that is, He permitted the perfect joy filling His soul to be manifested in His words.

When souls, with the aid of heavenly light, penetrate the mystery of the glory of God and with impassioned love seek and attain it, we can say, paraphrasing St. Francis of Assisi, that in this consists perfect joy.

The fulfillment of God's most holy Will gives Him glory. Abandonment to that Will accompanies love's deep desire to make the Beloved happy. When Jesus taught us to say: "Thy will be done on earth as it is in heaven," He expressed a directive for perfect joy.

But if we cannot make God happy in the full sense of

the term, because He Himself is substantial felicity, we can, indeed, make souls happy, and this lofty ideal is consonant with perfect love since charity embraces souls also.

This is the perfect joy of the Apostle: to make others happy by giving them temporal peace and eternal beautitude. Therefore, St. Paul called his children: "My joy and my crown"; therefore, St. John wrote: "Greater happiness than this I do not have, than to know that my children walk in the truth," as if he might say: "In this consists my perfect joy."

No joy resembles God's bliss more than bringing happiness to souls; nothing makes us more like Jesus than the fact that souls owe to us their eternal beautitude. To enlighten souls, to comfort, calm and sanctify them is truly perfect joy.

But there is another form of perfect joy, inward and supreme, because there is another form of perfect love.

The desire for union and the need of it reside in the very nature of love. St. Thomas teaches that union is the foundation, the essence and the aim of love. Charity is based upon the ineffable union between God and souls established by grace, for grace, being a participation in the divine nature, makes us of the same lineage as God. "For we are of His race," St. Paul declared boldly; and the disciple whom Jesus loved dared to say that the seed of God remains in the one born of Him.[5]

The essence of charity is the effective and holy union that puts into our souls the very sentiments of Jesus, according to the Apostle: "Let this mind be in you which is in Christ Jesus." The desire and the happiness of charity is the effective and perfect union with God, which inspired St.

Paul with these heavenly words: "I live now, not I, but Christ lives in me."

The plenitude of this union, undoubtedly, is attained in heaven where union is ineffably intimate, divinely beatifying, securely eternal; but love, impatient for God, does not wait for eternity to begin this most blessed union in souls. Like an anticipation of Paradise, love drops upon them some bits of beatitude that surpass all the pleasures of the senses and all the delights of earth.

When God unites Himself to souls with indescribable intimacy, inebriating them with the wine of His love, and when His deep, urgent longing is satisfied, who will doubt that those souls know perfect joy?[6]

That intimacy with God is an anticipation of heaven, the rehearsal of that triumphal entrance whose formula Jesus revealed to us: "Enter the joy of your Lord." The joy of the Lord is the infinite and most blissful union of the three Divine Persons, the inexpressible mystery of the life of God.

To each form of perfect love, then, corresponds a form of perfect joy.

To the perfect giving of the lover, which on earth is accomplished through suffering, corresponds the perfect joy that St. Francis of Assisi painted with a master's hand when he said that it consists in "suffering for the blessed Christ who desired so greatly to suffer for us."

To the good of the Beloved, the sole desire of perfect love, there corresponds in relation to God the soul's complacency in His infinite felicity and in loving abandonment to the divine Will; and in relation to the neighbor, the perfect joy of the apostle, which consists in making souls happy.

To the fullness of union, the supreme bliss of love, corresponds the entrance of the soul into the joy of the Lord, begun on earth with the ineffable intimacy of God for "those who know eternal life," and to be consummated in heaven.

If one considers it well, all these forms of perfect love are participations in the divine joy, for although God in His impassible nature does not experience the happiness of St. Francis of Assisi, it pleased the Divine Word to feel it abundantly in the human nature He assumed.

Perhaps also in the depth of all these forms of perfect joy there is hidden the same sorrow that appears so sublimely in one of them, for souls cannot be united with God unless they have been previously purified by pain; nor does love reach the heights of rest in God and of abandonment to the divine Will, unless sorrow has cleansed it from all human dross; neither can the apostle look upon his children as "his joy and his crown" until at the cost of indescribable afflictions the words of St. Paul have been realized: "I will spend all and I will spend myself for your souls."

Therefore, the Church in one of the Easter hymns, those liturgical hymns of perfect joy, intones this triumphal stanza:

> The Lamb's high banquet we await
> In snow-white robes of royal state;
> And now, the Red Sea's channel past,
> To Christ our Prince we sing at last.[7]

THE EASTER SEASON

ALLELUIA

THE EASTER SEASON

Chapter V

ALLELUIA

During the Easter season the Church never tires of repeating with loving satisfaction that mysterious canticle of joy which seems to be an echo of the chant of the blessed, "Alleluia!"

The Church, profoundly human, to relieve her unspeakable emotion at the remembrance of the triumph of her adorable Spouse, uses only one word, as happens in the great emotions of the human heart; but her spirit, which is the Spirit of God, pours into that word the unfathomable ocean of celestial happiness.

The Alleluia does not express earthly gladness, superficial and ephemeral; nor even that imperfect, spiritual joy that noble souls sometimes taste as a refreshment in the struggle, an encouragement in sorrow, or a presentiment of consummate joy; no, the joy of the *alleluia* is loftier, deeper, firmer; it is the reflection of Jesus' joy; it is the anticipation of heavenly happiness.

Joy is the fragrance of satisfied love, the cessation of desire, the ecstasy of possession, or contentment in the well-being of the Beloved. To each kind of love corresponds a joy: to the pitiable love of the world belongs its gilded gladness hiding corruption and emptiness; to human love belongs a happiness real but vain; such gladness does not fill the soul because the soul is immense; such gaiety ends in grief, as the Scripture says, because it is subject to human vicissitudes. To each victory of the soul in the spiritual life, to each God-given grace corresponds a spiritual joy—imperfect, however, because love is imperfect.

Perfect joy accompanies perfect love, that most pure love which, liberated from all egoism, seeks the good of the Beloved, God; and takes satisfaction therein. This is the exultation which the *alleluia* expresses, joy in His happiness, His triumph, His glory. It is the surpassing fragrance of perfect charity.

As joy is proportionate to love and to the good in which it delights, perfect happiness participates in the nature of the Infinite Good, that is, in His plenitude, His profundity, His strength.

Perfect joy is not subject to human vicissitudes. Does not the Church sing her victorious *alleluia* whatever the conditions of her human existence? Persecuted or triumphant, in the catacombs or on the throne, stained with the blood of martyrdom or resplendent with the light of victory, the Church always sings her *alleluia* during Paschal-tide; because all the vicissitudes of earth, however dolorous and terrible they may be, can neither destroy nor dim in the least the sublime, immortal fact that Jesus has risen, that He is happy, that He is encompassed with glory; because with God's light the Church looks upon persecutions and martyrdoms as real trifles, not worth the while of putting aside her heavenly joy.

Someone has said that since Jesus Christ arose joy should never disappear from the earth. In fact, what are these pains and griefs of ours, what do they signify before the colossal

during their exile these receive a certain fullness of the joy of Jesus.

The Church, most faithful spouse of Jesus and, in a certain sense, Jesus Himself, bears within her innermost heart perfect happiness, the joy of Jesus, and in spite of her constant martyrdoms, and through the strength itself of these martyrdoms, she feels the outburst of that joy which springs forth when the liturgical cycle commemorates and renews the glorious triumph of Jesus, and from her inspired lips and from her most tender heart arises the mysterious canticle of perfect joy: *Alleluia*!

THE EASTER SEASON

Easter Gladness

THE EASTER SEASON

Chapter VI

EASTER GLADNESS

"Rejoice in the Lord always;
again I say rejoice."[1]

When the Mass of Holy Saturday is celebrated with pontifical rite there is a deeply significant ceremony. After the Epistle has been read, the subdeacon approaches the bishop and in an especially solemn manner says: "Most Reverend Father, I announce to you a great joy, Alleluia!"[2]

Holy Church, as we know, does not exaggerate; she likes neither the pompous nor the theatrical; what she speaks is truth and she speaks it with a sincerity truly divine. If she announces a great joy which is expressed with this mysterious word, *Alleluia,* undoubtedly it is a reality; there is on the earth a great joy and this joy has as its own expression this word: *Alleluia.*

I dare to say that the joy which the Church proclaims to her children in this magnificent solemnity of the liturgical year is not simply a joy, it is *the joy,* "*the great joy,*" because it is a joy that, like our Lord Jesus Christ, is of yesterday, today, and of all ages; a joy that fills this day and swells to eternity; a joy that would be sufficient of itself alone to put an end to sadness on the earth and to fill all hearts with gladness.

In truth, how small appear our poverty, our shallowness, our fleeting afflictions before the immense, colossal, heavenly joy of the Resurrection of Our Lord Jesus Christ! How can we weep, however lacerated our heart may be, when Holy Church announces to us the great joy that is *Alleluia;* joy so great that it lays siege to all hearts, that it leaves no place for sadness and permits no tears but those of joy? Therefore, on this solemnity I wish to speak of that spiritual joy of which the Church speaks to us, and to say with St. Paul: "Rejoice in the Lord always; again I say, rejoice."

What are the motives for this immeasurable, absorbing joy, which leaves no place for sadness? There is only one motive: the Resurrection of Jesus. Jesus has risen, Jesus has triumphed over all His enemies; Jesus, glorious, resplendent, arose from the tomb to die no more, to triumph throughout the never-ending ages. This is the only and most firmly established object of the great joy that the Church declares to us and which ought to fill our Christian hearts.

The imperfection of our spirit is such that when we try to know one of God's mysteries we cannot take it in at a glance in its entirety; we tear it into bits, so to speak, in an effort to comprehend what is transcendental in this unique joy.

The formula that expresses Easter gladness is *alleluia.* Tobias pronounced this inscrutable word, foreseeing its evocation in a glorious Jerusalem. He predicted that *alleluia* would resound throughout that city's streets. St. John, in his apocalyptical visions, heard this mysterious paean in heaven. "I heard," he says, "a voice as it were of many multitudes saying in heaven, 'Alleluia' "; he relates to us that the echo of the divine song was continued and lost through endless ages, and that the symbolic ancients and the inhabitants of heaven repeated ceaselessly the secret canticle: "Amen, alleluia, alleluia; Amen, alleluia!"

But that alleluia, that mysterious hymn from heaven which the Church takes on her own lips and within her own heart to express the Easter joy has, in my judgment, many meanings: the alleluia of heaven, the alleluia of earth, and the interior alleluia of each heart. It always signifies a joy; it always signifies *the joy* with which Jesus Christ arose, with which He triumphed, the joy of the glorious, of the immortal.

The first meaning is this: The whole work that Our Lord Jesus Christ came to accomplish upon the earth and especially the sacrifice that His mortal life consummated can be expressed in these words of the Easter Sequence, that ingenuous sequence, full of poetry, which seems to hide in its stanzas some intangible, heavenly thing. In this sequence the sacrifice of Jesus is thus described: "'Together death and life in a strange conflict strove," and Life triumphed. Jesus Christ by dying triumphed over death and all His enemies, and His resurrection is His triumph of life over death, of good over evil, of truth over error, of God over demon; therefore we can say that the resurrection of Jesus Christ is the supreme triumph of history.

Oh, how small our poor victories appear in comparison with the triumph of Jesus Christ, Our Lord! Even the conquests of those soldiers of fortune in whose presence the world kept silent, the triumphs of Alexander, of Napoleon . . . how paltry they seem! Human victories are fleeting: the one who wins today, tomorrow dies of sorrow because his armies were routed . . . Oh, how fleeting are human gains . . . and how superficial! The most that a human triumph means is that one empire falls and another rises. But what is the exaltation of an empire beside that supreme, infinite triumph which embraces all history, which fills time and eternity: that triumph which Jesus Christ Our Lord attained when "death and life in a strange conflict strove."?

. . . Our victories are fragmentary; the triumph of Jesus Christ is a decisive, immortal victory. Therefore he is right who said that since Jesus Christ arose there should be no sadness upon earth. Thus the immortal problem of history, the problem of humanity, God's problem, has been solved definitively and gloriously; because God Who created us admirably, has reformed us even more admirably through Jesus Christ Our Lord. Therefore we should rejoice in our innermost heart, reiterating exultantly the glorious, unfathomable "*Alleluia.*"

But this is the first meaning of that glorious hymn, because the resurrection of Jesus Christ our Lord, verified nineteen centuries ago, is not, in a certain sense, something complete; it is something that in the course of the ages will keep on being fulfilled and which will be completed in the final days of time when the glory of God shines in all its splendor, when the heavens intone the glorious hymn, *Alleluia,* to be prolonged throughout the everlasting ages.

Let us remember what the Apostle Paul says to us: "I complete in my flesh what is lacking in the Passion of Jesus Christ." What is lacking in Jesus' Passion? If it was superabundant; if what He suffered was sufficient to redeem a thousand worlds; what was it that the Apostle St. Paul was going to complete in his frail flesh? The meaning of the expression of the Apostle is this: all the mysteries of Jesus have to be completed and perfected in us; because Jesus has not only a real body that was immolated on Calvary and that arose glorious after three days, but He has the Mystical Body, which we form.

Jesus, the complete Christ, is not only the one born of the Virgin Mary, but He is the one who keeps on being formed, year by year, century by century, epoch by epoch throughout history, until He returns to earth and incorporates with Himself the last of the predestined. Consequently, it is Jesus who lives, grows, speaks, suffers, dies, and triumphs in all the members of His Mystical Body. And thus history is nothing else than the prolongation of the Gospel.

It is plain that all Christ's mysteries are being completed constantly by us and that those mysteries will not be duly finished for God's glory and our happiness until the last day.

When history is judged superficially, we think that such a man of genius originated some universal movement among men, that he characterizes an historical epoch; or that such an event gives occasion to a certain shaping of the nations . . . This is only a superficial view; the profound judgment is that throughout the centuries, in the midst of all human vicissitudes, the work of God continues to be accomplished; and in every age Jesus speaks, Jesus is persecuted, Jesus is immolated, Jesus rises, and Jesus triumphs; and so history is but a series of Calvaries and a series of Easter days. It is a series of immolations of Jesus and of His Church and it is also a series of glorious triumphs.

Therefore the great joy that Holy Church announces to her children on this solemnity is not only the deed that was accomplished nineteen centuries ago, it is the joy of the deed that is always being accomplished . . . We ought to rejoice that Jesus Christ during nineteen centuries has risen without ceasing, because history after Christ can be expressed with the same stanza from the Easter Sequence: "Together death and life in strange conflict strove." They continue fighting because the mysteries of Jesus continue being fulfilled, and for nineteen centuries the immortal combat has been in progress on the earth and the outcome is ever the same:

> The Prince of life, who died,
> Now lives and reigns.

Jesus is ever dying, but He ever triumphs. He always rises, and this resurrection of Jesus in history that is realized throughout the ages and that must last until the end of time is the *great joy*: an ineffable joy that has an expression of deepest import: "Alleluia!" The interior joy that we feel in our hearts each year during the Paschal season is a sparkle of that great joy; and for us the inner gladness which occurs here in the depths of our souls has special importance. There, too, Jesus is rising just as He is arising in the world, as He arose nineteen centuries ago in Jerusalem.

The story of each soul is but a facsimile of the history of all humanity: a copy of the life of Jesus Christ. Here within our own heart Jesus reproduces His mysteries as He reproduces them in the Church of God. Within our heart He is born, in our heart He grows, in our heart He speaks, in our heart He immolates Himself, in our heart He triumphs, and those triumphs of Jesus Christ fill our soul with purest, celestial happiness.

For many Christians Easter is an indifferent joy, a day that has no meaning, a day like all the rest. They do not understand how the Church in her enthusiasm sings: "This is the day that the Lord has made; let us rejoice and be glad therein." The reason for this is that they have lost the sense of divine things. As the Apostle says: "Carnal man does not perceive the things of God." For men who have followed the lower instincts of their nature, who think of nothing but the fleeting goods of this world, and for those who have lost the habit of looking upwards, this day has no meaning.

For the Christian who has faith, hope, and love, for the one who lives the Christian life deeply and for whom Jesus Christ is the way, the truth, and the life, Easter is "the day that the Lord has made," the day of rejoicing and of gladness, because in the innermost heart of such a one, Jesus is triumphant. Here also there is battle—we know it very well. Within our heart there is a combat that we want to designate insignificant, because it deals with our frailty; but it is momentous because nothing less than the interests of God are struggling in the depths of our heart.

Like the history of the world, the story of each soul can be described in the stanza of the Easter Sequence: "Together death and life in a strange conflict strove." Has not our life been a constant struggle, an uninterrupted contest between life and death—between Jesus who desires to be in possession of our soul, and the devil who wishes to carry it away?

Thanks be to God that Jesus has triumphed in us! "The Lord of life, having died, now living, rules over the spoils from His enemies." That triumph of Jesus, His resurrection in the interior of our heart, produces a singular rejoicing which we express by that heavenly hymn: *Alleluia*!, the deep sentiment of our heart.

Let us pronounce in all its tones and with all its meanings the glorious hymn of the alleluia of triumph and of gladness; the alleluia of eternal happiness.

Let us forget our afflictions—they are so trifling; they are so superficial; they are so fleeting! What are they in comparison with the great joy that Holy Church announces to her children in the Easter season?

Let us forget our griefs, dry our tears, unite with all Christians on earth and all the blessed in heaven; and let us intone that mighty, glorious hymn, *Alleluia,* and may the reverberating notes of our canticle echo on into the endless ages of eternity. Amen.

THE PENTECOSTAL SEASON

The Feast of Pentecost

THE PENTECOSTAL SEASON

Chapter VII

The Feast of Pentecost

The feast of Pentecost closes the Easter season with supernal magnificence and opens a new stage in the liturgical life, a stage of union with God, of perfect living, of renewal, of fervor.

Upon ascending into heaven Christ did not leave us in exile, abandoned and orphaned; He sent us His Spirit, the Spirit of Truth and of Love, of Counsel and of Fortitude.

The Holy Spirit is the gift of God, the gift par excellence, from whom come all the graces that God lavishes upon souls, life-giving streams that give perpetual vigor to the Church.

Fruit of all the merits of Christ and most perfect consummation of His work, the descent of the Holy Spirit came about to renew the earth, to inflame hearts and to sanctify souls.

Christ had sown throughout the world the seed of His word, but this seed did not germinate until the Holy Spirit fertilized it; Christ left on earth the spark of love that had to be lighted up, but this fire burned only when fanned with the breath of the Holy Spirit; Christ, by opening His Heart, opened the inexhaustible fountain of life, but the Holy Spirit must pour out this life into hearts, communicating Himself to them in a wonderful way.

In the Apostles, especially, the heirs of the priesthood of Christ, the Holy Spirit wrought a marvellous transformation: they were ignorant and they became wise; they were cowards and He filled them with strength; they were self-centered and their hearts became possessed by love, abnegation and heroism.

Has the Holy Spirit lost His efficacy? No, it would be blasphemous to think so. Has He discontinued pouring Himself into souls? By no means; He communicates Himself to us in baptism and He lavishes His fruitful abundance upon us in Confirmation. Year by year on the feast of Pentecost He renews in souls the effects that He produced in the souls of the Apostles, communicating Himself to the hearts of the faithful, especially to those devoted to Him. He is still our comfort and our strength.

How many times upon considering the abyss of our misery and the immensity of our obligations we feel disconsolate and hopeless! We should not fear; we rely on the same strength that made the Apostles invincible; the Spirit of Christ is our spirit. If we dispose our souls to receive this Spirit of Truth, of Love and of Consolation, He will transform our hearts as He transformed the hearts of the first faithful and, in spite of our wretchedness, we shall continue accomplishing upon the earth the work of peace and of holiness begun by Christ.

Let us be devoted to the Holy Spirit and in that devotion we shall find the strength and the joy to fulfill our arduous duties.

THE PENTECOSTAL SEASON

Come, Holy Spirit

THE PENTECOSTAL SEASON

Chapter VIII

Come, Holy Spirit

The number of times that the Church calls upon the Holy Spirit is noteworthy. "Come, Holy Ghost!" "Come, Creator Spirit blest!" "Come, Thou Father of the poor!" "Come, Thou Comforter!" "Come! Come!" Always: "Come!" —the word of desire, the word of human love.

In the long centuries that preceded the coming of Christ, "Come" was the cry of humanity awaiting the Savior, the supplication of the patriarchs and the prophets, the half-understood, half-formulated desire of those who were sitting in darkness and in the shadow of death.

Another more inward and ardent desire was the plea of Mary and of the Apostles during the nine days in the Cenacle when they awaited the Advocate, the Holy Spirit promised by Christ. True advent of the Holy Spirit, that brief period contained greater depths of love and of hope than the long-delayed advent of Christ. It sufficed that Mary was there!

The supplication of the Church while time endures is exactly the same: "Come!" *Come*, the last word to be heard in time, the word that closes Scripture, the word that will end history, the word that will open heaven! "And the Spirit and the bride say, "Come!" And let him who hears say, 'Come'."[1]

What is the nature and efficacy of this desire, the profound significance of this word *Come*?

The distinctive character of human love is desire. While we live on this earth, to live and to desire are for us one and the same thing. "Man is a nothing that thirsts," Monsignor Gay has said, "that desire is our greatness, the only infinite thing within us."

Even among holy souls who attain here on earth that most blessed possession, divine union, those who love the more are those who desire the more. Union with God, in proportion to its intimacy, keeps expanding the heart and deepening desire up to the summit of sanctity, the height of love and of union. There love is a sweet, glorious martyrdom; but, after all, it is a martyrdom, the martyrdom of love. If there is rest on those heights, it is not the repose of possession, but the cessation of desire, as St. Thomas taught; the repose of the heart that having gathered its desires before being scattered has unified and simplified them in one supreme desire that only in heaven will attain the repose of possession. "They that eat Me shall yet hunger; and they that drink Me shall yet thirst."[2]

Can it be that desire is the mysterious bond that unites suffering and love upon the earth?

It is certain that the desire of our heart has a decisive power over the Sacred Heart; it does Him great violence; it might be said that He cannot resist our desires. When He wants to grant us a grace, He first of all inspires us with the desire of it, and perhaps it is the only disposition that He requires of us; because humility is the root of desire and prayer is the delicate perfume that it exhales.

The time of the coming of the Messiah was revealed to Daniel by the Archangel because he was a "man of desires."[3]

Solomon desired wisdom and it came to him: "Wherefore I wished, and understanding was given to me; and I called upon God and the Spirit of Wisdom came upon me."[4] Desire prolonged the life of the old man Simeon so that he might see the salvation of the Lord; and neither human nor angelic language can ever explain how unspeakably profound was Mary's desire when she received the celestial tidings of the Incarnation of the Word.

"Open thy mouth wide and I will fill it,"[5] says the Lord in the Old Testament.

"Blessed are they who hunger and thirst after justice for they shall be satisfied,"[6] said the Divine Master upon promulgating the code of the New Law in the sermon on the Mount.

"Therefore, desire of wisdom bringeth to the everlasting kingdom;"[7] the desire for Christ, the Wisdom of the Father, leads to the eternal kingdom.

What more can be said of the efficacy of desire? Prayer, whose omnipotent power the entire Scripture proclaims, proceeds from desire, like the fragrant spiral of incense triumphantly mounting heavenward from the glowing coals. Prayer is desire, desire with the mystic sweetness of its perfumes.

Tears, too, whose cry is irresistible, are also the incarnation of desire for they are either the fruit of sorrow or the sweet flowering of tenderness.

To desire sanctity is to begin to be a saint; to desire love is already to love; to desire happiness is to have found the road that leads thereto. Therefore, the Church, possessing the Holy Spirit, Soul of her soul, and desiring to possess Him still more, calls to Him: "Come! Come!"

Likewise souls who know the gift of God prepare themselves for the feast of Pentecost, repeating the most sacred word "*Come*!" They say it with their lips, they reiterate it with their heart, their tears, their blood, and with their works, which are also their desires because they are the petitioning for the final master-work, the accomplishment that is no longer desire, but rather possession—the living, unending masterpiece of beatitude.

May our souls be transformed into desire, into a single, consuming, divinely inspired desire, and God will send us the Holy Spirit, His Gift, His Love!

Veni, Sancte Spiritus!

THE PENTECOSTAL SEASON

Father of the Poor

THE PENTECOSTAL SEASON

Chapter IX

Father of the Poor

The Pentecostal liturgy is exceedingly beautiful. Two hymns are especially marvellous: the well known *Veni Creator Spiritus* sung at Vespers and at Tierce, and the Sequence of the Pentecost Mass, repeated through the octave. In these hymns are found exquisite beauty, precious invocations and supplications full of unction. It would be worth while to meditate on the different pleadings, the several stanzas of these hymns, because our piety would certainly find here abundant spiritual benefit.

I wish to glean from that field, and I select three words, *Veni, Pater Pauperum*: a simple invocation but one very rich in meaning, which, with the help of the same Holy Spirit, I shall explain on this occasion of the feast of Pentecost. In the Sequence of the Mass, the Church in the midst of other invocations, addresses the Holy Spirit with these words: "*Come, Father of the Poor*!"

I think that this invocation is plainly a consoling one: "Come, Father of the poor!" Holy Church evidently is not referring to those who lack the goods of fortune; the word *poor* does not have the usual connotation that we give it in daily life, it treats of poverty in the spiritual order.

The poor are those whose heart is detached, whose soul

is desolate, who thirst for love, who struggle with their own miseries and frailty; therefore it goes without saying that we are all poor. Who does not hide an anxiety, a desire, a thirst in the depths of the soul? Some seek peace; others, love; some, light and rest.

We are all poor by the very limitations of our nature; poor, because by our sins we have squandered the precious heritage that we received from God; poor, because in this sorrowful vale of tears, we long to possess those spiritual riches lacking in our fallen nature. We are all poor, but what happiness, what comfort to know that the Holy Spirit is the Father of the poor! Scripture and the Church show us the marvels that the Holy Spirit has accomplished upon the earth. In the beginning of time He moved over chaos, over that formless, empty earth: "The Spirit of God moved over the waters," the Book of Genesis tells us. And upon passing over chaos, He transformed it marvellously—putting into it light, order, beauty, life.

In the fullness of time, the Holy Spirit descended upon the most holy Virgin in Nazareth, overshadowed her, and the fruit of that coming of the Holy Spirit is nothing less than Jesus, our Savior; Jesus, He who encompasses within Himself the charms of heaven and of earth; Jesus, our life, our hope, our peace, our love and our happiness.

On the day of Pentecost, the Holy Spirit descended into the Cenacle upon the Apostles who were gathered there in union with Mary, most holy, and when He descended upon them He transformed them, sanctified them, divinized them and created the Church, the Kingdom of God upon the earth.

Indeed, whenever the Holy Spirit descends, He performs something very extraordinary. He descends upon chaos and forms the world; He descends upon Mary and forms Jesus; He descends upon the Apostles and forms a Church, the Kingdom of God. When He descends, He comes to bring light and life, to bring peace and love.

But there will always be some one who says: "Who would be worthy to have the Holy Spirit descend into his soul?"

At first sight one might think that the Holy Spirit descends only upon chosen souls. He descended upon Mary most holy, the pure, the immaculate; He descended upon the Apostles, the predestined ones, those who were going to continue the mission of Jesus Christ, those who were to achieve a mighty work upon the earth. But upon us, so small, so miserable, so sinful, with empty hearts and desolate souls; why would the Holy Spirit descend upon us? Happy the sinless souls! Happy the saints! Happy those who living in recollection and in contemplation and in the sacred silence of love, receive supernal gifts from the Paraclete!

But we? We *have* the right and the hope of receiving the Holy Spirit! Do we know why? Because He is the Father of the poor and we are poor. The smaller our soul, the deeper our misery, the more pitiable our heart, the better right and title we have to the descent of the Spirit of God upon us.

After meditating deeply upon these words, I do not find that the Holy Spirit is the support or the succor of the poor, but their *Father*. Here on earth the poor feel satisfied when they find a generous heart, a munificent hand, when they meet someone who has compassion on their misery and succors them; but the Holy Spirit is not the support of the poor, He does not have pity on them; ah, no! He is their Father, He loves them.

Do we understand how much consolation lies in this expression of the Church: *"Father of the poor"*? If I am poor, I hold in my hand the credential for invoking the Holy Spirit. If I were spiritually rich, if my soul were adorned with magnificent virtues, if I possessed bountiful gifts of God in my heart, I would not have the confidence that I now have in invoking the Holy Spirit and in hoping that He may come to my soul. But because He is the Father of the poor I present to Him the immense need of my soul, and I invoke Him with the Church, "Come, Father of the poor," and I am sure that He will come to me and will enrich me with His gifts.

Yes, I know that He will come because I am poor, because I am ignorant; I shall show Him the credential of my wretchedness and my deficiencies, I shall show Him my wounds and I shall open my heart to Him, and I am sure that my very misery, my smallness, my failings will make Him come!

If we reflect upon the comings of the Holy Spirit, we shall find that whenever He has come to earth He has descended upon wretchedness, upon smallness, and upon nothingness.

We have just spoken of three marvellous comings of the Holy Spirit to earth. The first, when in the beginning of time, He descended upon chaos, He passed over that abyss, transforming it and made rise from it this world filled with order and harmony and beauty.

The Holy Spirit descended upon another chaos when He descended upon the Apostles in the Cenacle. The Apostles who were gathered in the Cenacle were not rich, they were poor like ourselves, they had many spiritual limitations. Do we not remember how the Apostles all fled in the tragic moments of the Passion? St. John scarcely appears on Mount Calvary at the foot of the Cross in union with the holy Virgin Mary. Peter himself, the Prince of the Apostles, denied the Master three times on the night of the Passion.

That the Apostles were poor is evident from the Gospels: In the Cenacle, when Our Lord Jesus Christ was presenting the mighty marvels of the heavenly kingdom, when He was instituting the Holy Eucharist, when He was speaking to the hearts of the Apostles, telling them His innermost secrets, were they not discussing who would be the greatest in the kingdom of heaven? Ignorant, ungrateful, cowardly, such were the Apostles. And over the chaos of those miseries, the Holy Spirit descended on the day of Pentecost and transformed it, making them valiant men, full of zeal and of wisdom so that they spread throughout the whole world the doctrine of Jesus.

And even when the Holy Spirit descended upon the Blessed Virgin Mary, He descended no doubt upon a spotless, immaculate creature, upon a very saintly soul, but the Virgin reveals to us a secret and tells us that, in the midst of those graces with which Our Lord enriched her, she carried deep within, her smallness, her lowliness, her nothingness. "Because He hath regarded the lowliness of His handmaid: for behold, from henceforth all nations shall call me blessed."

Do we understand that it is always pleasing to the Holy Spirit to descend upon chaos, upon misery, upon smallness? Do we understand that the Holy Spirit is really the Father of the poor? How our heart expands and how our soul is filled with consolation, knowing perfectly well that our own limitations and lowliness are valuable credentials for invoking the Holy Spirit, making Him descend into our hearts! Is He not infinite Love, the substantial Love of the Father?

He is not a Spirit who descends only to holy souls and chosen hearts, no; His pleasure is to be in souls that thirst, in hearts that are detached, in all those who are in need and who sigh for the love and the peace and the happiness of heaven. We have, consequently, the right to have the Holy Spirit descend upon us in spite of our ingratitude, our misery, our failings. To speak out my thought completely, it is precisely on account of our ingratitude and our misery that we have the right to the coming of the Spirit of God, infinite Love, justly called by the Church the "Father of the poor."

But it is fitting to note more carefully an idea which I have already expressed. The Holy Spirit is not simply a support, He is not only a succor of the poor, He is their *Father*. The difference is evident. There are on earth generous men who pity the miseries of the poor, and assist them liberally. But these may not have love for the poor man, they have compassion for him; they give him their material resources, their sincere sympathy, but nothing more.

The Holy Spirit is not like that; He is not only a most generous God who lavishes His gifts everywhere, because He has compassion upon His poor creatures, no; He is a Father, and the Father loves, the father gives his son what his son needs, but above all these gifts, he gives his heart, he gives his love. He does not feel pity for his son, he feels tenderness.

What a difference there is between a protector and a father, between a generous man who pities us and a noble man who loves us! The Holy Spirit is the "Father of the poor," that is, He loves us, He comes to us with love. He does not come impelled by something that we might conceive as a kind of duty; He does not come through compassion for our destitution. He comes full of love, He comes to us because He is Father of the poor, and, since He is our Father He draws near full of tenderness and pours into our souls His divine gifts. Above all His gifts, He gives us His love, or to speak more exactly, those gifts are impregnated with the supreme gift of Himself, with the supreme gift of His love.

I repeat, how consoling is this invocation which the Holy Church places on our lips during the octave of Pentecost! The Holy Spirit is the "Father of the poor." Let us so invoke Him, because this character of "Father of the poor" fills our hearts with confidence. No longer shall we have to say: "Blessed the stainless souls, blessed the saintly ones, blessed those who have prepared for this most solemn feast in recollection and in love! But rather, blessed the poor, blessed the lowly, blessed the souls that thirst for love! The Holy Spirit will descend upon them, because the Holy Spirit is the 'Father of the poor'."

O Holy Spirit, the Paraclete! Spirit who proceeds from the Father and the Son and who have poured out yourself upon every creature, scattering everywhere light, love and unction! We know that when You descend to earth, You come to accomplish marvels; that You created a world when You descended upon chaos in the beginning of time; that You formed Jesus when You descended upon the lowliness of the Virgin Mary; that You created a Church when nineteen centuries ago You descended upon the Apostles in the Cenacle.

O Divine Spirit! Come, come and transform our poor souls! See how poor we are! In our hands we bring the titles and the credentials for obliging You to come; our credentials are our smallness, our wretchedness, our failings.

Lord, we are poor, immensely poor; see our empty hearts, our desolate souls, and our deep desires.

Lord, we are poor and You are not only the support of the poor, You are the "Father": You do not have mere compassion on us, You have love for us. Come, then, descend upon us! O Divine Spirit, brood over the chaos of our smallness and of our misery, then everything will be regenerated and You will transform our hearts and our lives.

Transform us, Lord! Make of us something beautiful, something luminous, something full of harmony, or rather make us a copy of Jesus, of that Jesus whom You formed in the immaculate womb of the Virgin Mary. O Father of the poor, descend upon the chaos of our souls, fill them with love, for You are infinite love, and transform our smallness and our meanness, making of us a replica of Jesus!

THE PENTECOSTAL SEASON

The Paraclete

THE PENTECOSTAL SEASON

Chapter X

The Paraclete

The name *Paraclete* is frequently applied to the Holy Spirit in Scripture and in the liturgy.

Our Lord Jesus Christ, at the Last Supper on that night of holy disclosures and final confidences, spoke freely to the disciples about the Holy Spirit as a comfort, a hope, and He designated Him with this mysterious name: "I will ask the Father and He will give you another Paraclete to dwell with you forever."[1] "But the Paraclete, the Holy Spirit whom the Father will send in My name, will teach you all things."[2]

The Church caught that sweet name from the lips of her Spouse and she uses it often with delicate confidence. "Thou who art called the Paraclete," she sings in the *Veni Creator*, a most beautiful hymn, a marvel of love and of devotion; she speaks of the Paraclete in the doxology of innumerable liturgical hymns; in the Collect of the Pentecost Mass she begs that we may enjoy the consolations of the Spirit, of Him whom she addresses in a masterly Sequence as "Thou of comforters the best."[3]

Consoling must be a very important function of the Holy Spirit since on that account He receives the name of Paraclete.

And in truth, if there is anything necessary and desirable

in this life, it is consolation. We have such great need of it! One would say that it is what we need most on this earth because sorrow surrounds us unremittingly, for it issues from our own innermost self; we breathe an atmosphere of misery and grief.

Man does not comfort, he does not know how to comfort; man can do many things, he can persuade and he can move, he can sympathize and he can love; but he is ignorant of the secret of consolation. In the presence of sorrow he feels an incredible powerlessness, and if at times he succeeds in pouring a drop of comfort into a broken heart it is because he possesses something god-like; the one who is comforting is not the man, he is the instrument of God.

Consolation is, doubtless, a very lofty thing; but I think that the office of drying our tears in the countless superficial griefs that form the accidents of life would not suffice to give to the Holy Spirit that title as constituting His primal function.

One must have a more profound and transcendental sorrow, one must have a grief that is not accidental, but established in the very basis of human nature. The consolation of the Paraclete must needs correspond to this deep rooted sorrow. I find that sorrow in the pages of Scripture and in the depths of my own heart.

"The sparrow hath found for herself a house, and the turtle a nest where she may lay her young ones,"[4] exclaims the Psalmist, concealing something very deep in that masterly reticence. Those words make me feel the very vivid contrast between the complete peace of nature and the incessant inquietude of the human heart.

Everything in nature has an intense character of quiet and of calm: the stars travel their long, mysterious paths which the hand of God marked out for them with an incomparable peace, with a contagious peace, for it suffices to gaze at the star-studded sky to be possessed of peace; every day the sun rises on the horizon in the midst of the rejoicing of the dawn and plunges into the glory of the sunset with indescribable calm, with sweet peace; the flowers open tranquilly, scatter their aroma and fade away sweetly, exhaling their most exquisite fragrance when they are dying. Everything in nature is quiet; the little bird finds her warm shelter hidden in a rock; the turtle-dove, her nest where she hides her little ones . . . Only the heart of man is unceasingly agitated, grieved by a most painful longing, tortured by a poignant anguish.

This longing takes several forms and receives many names: in the wicked it is desperation; in the imperfect, anxiety; in the saints, desire that at times is changed into martyrdom; but it is always the same, the perpetual scourge of the human heart.

Can it be the sweet nostalgia for Paradise? Can it be the seal, the heavenly seal that the Lord put upon our souls when He raised us to a supernatural order? I do not know; but no one will be able to draw out of us that desire for God, the thirst for God, the imperious need for God.

When this desire is fulfilled forever in the plenitude of joy, we shall have the glory of the fatherland; when here on earth we possess God, as far as the limitations of our exile permit, we shall have the deep consolation, the holy comfort that the Paraclete pours into our hearts.

How is this prodigy of comfort accomplished?

That we in exile may possess God intimately, that we may carry Him as a divine treasure in the fragile vessel of our being, that we may see with His eyes, love with His

Heart, breathe with his breath, and live with His life, this is a lesson that Christ Himself taught us expressly. Consider these inspiring words calculated to make us saints provided we penetrate their meaning: "If any one love Me he will keep My words, and My Father will love Him, and We will come to him and make our abode with him.[5]

Our heart can be a heaven because the august Trinity can fill it with its greatness.

But let us delve into the mystery, now that the gentle Master has discovered to us the secrets of God in the pages of the Holy Gospel, which were written not only for theologians and scholars but for all men of good will.

Jesus reveals to us in these sacred pages the character and the order of our relations with the three divine Persons. "No one comes to the Father but through Me."[6] To go to the Father, to feel His loving caresses, His infinite tenderness, to bask in His gaze—that look of beatitude with which He sees the Word—to go to the Father is the height of perfection and of happiness. To go to the Father there is only one path: the Incarnate Word. United to Christ, incorporated with Christ, members of His Body, branches of the Mystical Vine, we enter through Him, with Him and in Him, into the very life of the Trinity, into the joy of the Lord; united to the Word, the Father will see us with the same look with which He contemplates His Son, He will love us with the same infinite love with which He loves Him, and we shall see the Father with the eyes of the Word and we shall love Him with His infinite Heart.

The way to go to the Father is Christ; but the Holy Spirit accomplishes the mystery of our incorporation into Christ.

As the Holy Spirit is the bond of love between the

Father and the Son, so also is He the gentle tie that unites our soul with the Word. Who but Love, infinite, personal Love, must work those miracles of union whose fullness Christ prayed for on the night of the Last Supper, saying: "That they may be one even as We are one: I in them and Thou in Me; that they may be perfected in unity."[7]

Until the Holy Spirit was infused into souls, the work of Christ appeared incomplete and sterile, as it were. Men heard the words of the Master without understanding them; they perceived the sweet charms of Jesus without being inflamed with divine love; they approached the fountain of life without drinking. It was necessary that the Holy Spirit come, and, giving Himself to us, unite our souls with Jesus and diffuse in them the charity of God, the grace of God, the divine communication of God. "The charity of God is poured forth in our hearts by the Holy Spirit who has been given to us."[8]

The Holy Spirit, giving Himself to us, brings us the plenitude of the divine gift; He brings us the Most Holy Trinity, with divine consolation He fills the void in our souls: He is the Paraclete.

What He gives is not yet the interminable joy, the glorious bliss of the fatherland; it is the nostalgia of exile, yet it is secure peace. It is the interior calm of the soul, a sweet, strengthening unction that floods our faculties, bathing our entire being, like the delicate, abundant aromatic oil that poured down the beard of Aaron, running down his garment until it reached the hem of his cloak.

The miseries of life, the superficial griefs, the Paraclete comforts or not, according to His pleasure. How often saints endure bitter sorrows! The Sanctifier however floods the soul with consolation. This explains the striking contrast observed in the saints; judged exteriorly, it might be said that they are the most unhappy beings on earth—they suffer so much! But hidden within their soul is the sacred secret of comfort, joy and peace. "In the sight of the unwise they seemed to die; but they are in peace."[9]

Paraclete is the name given to the Divine Spirit in this sad exile; in the fatherland He has another essential name, a divine name: He is called *Love*.

The Paraclete consoles; Love glorifies; the Paraclete pours balm into hearts; Love inebriates souls with the new wine of happiness. The Church, filled with God-given consolations, sighs for the eternal fatherland; on Pentecost she cries out to the Holy Spirit with the sweet melancholy, and the precious unction that her words always bear when she speaks of heaven: "Grant to us the reward of virtue, the attainment of salvation, and everlasting joy."[10]

THE PENTECOSTAL SEASON

Sources of Joy

THE PENTECOSTAL SEASON

Chapter XI

SOURCES OF JOY

The final word of Christianity is joy. However noble, however fruitful, however holy suffering may be, it is nothing more than a means—a precious means—it is nothing more than a path—a blessed path—through which one arrives at joy and happiness.

The Apostle St. Paul expresses this doctrine to us with his usual mastery of phrase. He speaks thus of Christ: "... who for the joy set before Him, endured a cross."[1] The Cross so dear to His Heart, whereon He wanted to affix life, salvation and hope, is the divine means to attain a joy unexplained by the Apostle, but yet one not only for Jesus, but for us especially. With His sufferings, humiliations, and sorrows Christ purchased joy for us.

On the eve of His Passion He said to His disciples: "I have told you these things so that My joy may remain with you and your joy be complete." He taught us what we must do to attain happiness; He suffered and died for us so that we might have perfect joy, that joy which neither anything nor any one ever can tear away from us. Therefore, Holy Church always rejoices, even in the hour of trial, even in the midst of the most terrible persecutions.

One of the characteristics of the Catholic liturgy is joy.

Every day Holy Church invites us to prayer at the beginning of the Divine Office and at Matins with the glad summons: "Come, let us rejoice in the Lord; let us joyfully sing to God our Savior."[2] Even in the sad, austere Office of Good Friday the cry of joy resounds when the crucifix is uncovered and elevated.

Although our entire liturgy is impregnated with joy, there are three tremendous outbursts of gladness during the liturgical year.

The first occurs on the night of the Nativity; it is the cry of sweet, ingenuous, child-like joy; it is the gladness of dawn, the rejoicing of spring, the happiness of infancy. In the midst of the angels' song Jesus appears upon the manger straw trembling with cold, radiant with love, and we, upon contemplating Him with enlightened minds, feel that He imparts to us a heavenly happiness.

The second mighty outpouring of joy is the solemn and triumphant jubilation of the Resurrection. When we reflect that Jesus Christ, conqueror of sin and death, arose from the sepulcher in glorified beauty, our being thrills with happiness as we chant the *Alleluia,* that mysterious canticle which expresses the gladness of heaven descended to earth.

The third revelation of joy is the ecstasy of Pentecost: perhaps more profound, more complete, but also more hidden than the Easter gladness. Holy Church speaks to us of this joy in the Preface of the Mass. In this very important part of the liturgy, Holy Church is accustomed to express what is most noteworthy in the spirit of each solemnity; we might say that in the Prefaces we find, the quintessence, as it were, of the liturgical spirit of the day. The Pentecostal Preface, after affirming that Jesus Christ, ascended into heaven and seated at the right hand of the Father, sent the

Holy Spirit upon His adopted sons, adds: "Wherefore does the whole world rejoice with exceeding great joy."

And so it should be: the joy of the Resurrection is the gladness of triumph; the rejoicing of one who enjoys tranquilly and sweetly the fruits of victory. On Calvary Jesus conquered sin and death, but the fruit of that divine sacrifice was the outpouring of the Holy Spirit upon all souls. Pentecost is the consummation of all the mysteries of Christ. Pentecost is the definitive triumph, the consummate victory. Therefore, on this day, when the Spirit of God descends upon the earth, the whole world trembles with jubilation and with joy.

The happiness of God, His personal happiness, is the Holy Spirit; He is the joy of heaven; He is the joy of earth. Jesus tells us that the Kingdom of God is justice, peace and joy in the Holy Spirit. Does not the Scripture speak to us on several occasions of that joy of the Holy Spirit, signifying, as it were, that joy is something proper to Him?

I wish to speak of this interior, supernatural joy; I wish to impress this truth that the Holy Spirit is the cause of our joy, that it is characteristic of Him to spread happiness wherever He goes; I wish to analyze this heavenly joy of Pentecost. When speaking of holy matters we need to analyze them, and although it may seem that analysis detracts from the mysterious reality, nevertheless, it is impossible to study sacred mysteries in any other way.

Pentecostal gladness is composed of three exalted types of joy poured out upon the world and into hearts by the Holy Spirit: the joy of *purity*, the joy of *love*, the joy of *sacrifice*.

The world, the frivolous, deceitful world, falsifies joy as it counterfeits everything; its happiness is of tinsel, ordinarily hiding sadness and emptiness. The world does not understand that joy can be found in purity; perhaps it thinks that to be happy in life it is necessary to allow the heart an unlimited freedom, that it is indispensable to permit all our instincts and evil propensities to develop fully. But that is not so; purity produces happiness.

At first glance we think that the saints are very sad. They lower their eyes, they keep silence, they seek recollection, they are mortified, so we believe that the life of the saints is sorrowful; nevertheless, they all speak to us of joy.

St. Paul exclaims: "I abound with joy in the midst of my tribulations." St. Francis Xavier asked God not to pour so many consolations into his soul, because he could no longer support such great happiness. St. Thérèse of the Child Jesus, with her holy simplicity, tells us when she was near death: "I found happiness and joy upon the earth."

It is the happiness of purity. If heaven is eternal joy, it is because heaven is the abode of purity; nothing stained may enter there, all is pure because all is divine.

Paradise was a replica of heaven before original sin was committed. If Adam and Eve had remained in their primal grace, Paradise would have remained an abode of happiness; under its luxuriant foliage sadness would never have found shelter. When sin was committed, sorrow entered the world; and during long centuries, happiness, like a lightning flash, has scarcely shone from time to time upon the earth.

When Jesus came as a babe in Bethlehem, the angels intoned over the manger the song of gladness. "Peace to men of good will," is the harbinger of the divine joy that would reign upon the earth.

Because Jesus brought us purity, He therefore brought

us joy. And it is the Holy Spirit who diffuses purity into hearts.

Do we know what purity is? Ordinarily we have an incomplete idea of it because we view it under a negative aspect: we think that purity is simply the lack of stain, the preservation from evil. No, purity is something positive, purity is God and His reflection in creatures; pure souls are those who reflect God.

I think that souls are like crystals. In a crystal there is an enormous capacity for light; in a soul there is a great capacity for the divine; when that soul is filled with celestial light, when grace inundates her, then that soul is pure.

No soul is more pure, after that of Our Lord Jesus Christ, than the soul of the Blessed Virgin; it is a marvel of purity because it is full of grace, because Our Lord put into her a full measure of the divine.

The Holy Spirit, upon entering our souls brings, we might say, two kinds of purity: infinite purity and created purity; infinite purity, because He gives Himself to dwell in us; He is the gift of God. Upon coming to us, He pours into our souls grace with its cortege of gifts and virtues; this is created purity.

Wherever the Holy Spirit is found, there is purity; the purity of heaven and the purity of earth. The soul that receives the Holy Spirit has grace, which is created purity, and it has infinite purity, which is God. Therefore, when the Holy Spirit is poured into our soul, the *whole world rejoices* because a tremendous torrent of purity has filled souls, and with purity, joy has come to the world.

The second form of joy that the Holy Spirit produces in hearts is the joy of love. It is easier to understand that love produces happiness. Joy is, indeed, the special fruit of love;

in the same way that flowers have their individual perfume, so the fragrance of this divine flower of charity is joy.

Poor human love suffices to fill hearts with happiness, especially when it is deep and noble. Is not earthly love a very fountain of joy?

But heavenly love, divine love especially, produces joy. Yet, relative to love, much is said of suffering; and certainly love and sorrow are intimately connected upon this earth; but despite this intimate, mysterious bond, love always results in happiness. Hence, as I have said before, joy is the final word of Christianity, because the foundation of Christianity is charity.

What else is joy but the sanctification of our innermost aspirations, the expansion of heart that we feel when love is reciprocated? The Holy Spirit is eternal, infinite love. He is the personal love of God; therefore, I stated that the Holy Spirit is the joy of heaven, because He is the love of the Father and of the Son; and when this divine love is lavished upon the earth, when we are inflamed by the fire of that volcano of love, we experience a new joy because we experience a new love.

What a pity that we are so dull in comprehending divine things! Ordinarily earthly things arouse us, they attract our energy, they captivate our faculties but in the face of current affairs we can with difficulty contemplate immortal, divine things.

If we could make a reality of that supernatural world which Christ came to establish upon the earth and which is hidden under the coarse wrappings of the material world; if we could contemplate the prodigies of God's love in hearts and the heavenly affections that it inspires, we would understand how the fragrance of that blessed flower of charity is happiness. We would understand how happiness has been established in the world since charity was established, since the Holy Spirit descended upon the Apostles on the day of Pentecost. That effusion was not fleeting, it was not passing, it is everlasting.

The life of the Church is an uninterrupted Pentecost; the Holy Spirit constantly descends upon souls filling, warming and inflaming them with the fire of charity. Then, like a delightful perfume or an unearthly incense, holy joy rises up from their very depths.

The Holy Spirit lavishes upon the earth another form of joy: the joy of suffering. At first sight the joy of suffering seems a paradox. Is there not a contradiction between these two terms? Can sorrow and happiness be joined in one heart? Is not grief precisely the constant, victorious enemy of our gladness?

It is indeed, possible for joy and sorrow to be united in one heart; in the Sacred Heart they were united. Christ endured tremendous sorrows not only during the short hours of the Passion, but His whole life was a cross and a martyrdom. At the same time, throughout His life He carried, as some one said "a secret in His Heart," the secret of His joy.

The happiness of Jesus Christ was the happiness of heaven. His sorrow was comparable to the sorrow of hell. Wonderful, divine paradox, how in the Sacred Heart the gladness of heaven could be associated with a sorrow resembling, in a certain way, the sorrow of hell.[3]

With due proportion guarded, joy and sorrow can be united in Christian hearts, too. Does not the Apostle St. Paul tell us: "I overflow with joy in all our troubles."[4] The Apostle endured heavy griefs but he likewise knew a surpassing happiness.

It is fitting that we examine with greater attention these intimate relations between joy and sorrow.

The first wonder that the Holy Spirit works in the world is to preserve joy in our heart in the midst of sorrow. Therefore He is called, on occasions, the Comforter.

We may define consolation as joy in the midst of sorrow. When we are heart-broken, if some one knocks at our door and comes to pour into our stricken heart a drop of love, we experience consolation, a gladness in spite of suffering.

The Holy Spirit is the Paraclete, the Comforter; in the midst of our griefs He pours into our heart a heavenly comfort, a divine consolation; He has the secret of consoling. He knows how to pour out some drops of joy in the midst of our sorrows and tribulations; all souls who suffer in a Christian manner experience this relief.

No, Jesus did not come to destroy suffering. He did not come to end its reign; Jesus loves suffering and He made of it an instrument of His power and His glory. He came to consecrate it, to transform it into a sacred happiness; the cross, the emblem of suffering is the symbol of Christianity.

Christ did not destroy sorrow; He revealed to us the secret of consolation so that we could carry our cross with joy.

The Apostle St. Peter speaks of the joy in sharing the sufferings of Christ: ". . . rejoice, in so far as you are partakers of the sufferings of Christ, that you may also rejoice with exultation in the revelation of His glory."[5] It is the Holy Spirit who inspires this blessed joy into hearts because He is the Comforter.

But this is not the only relation that exists between sorrow and joy. Suffering is ordinarily the path that leads to true happiness.

The formula of St. Paul of which I have already spoken can be applied to us also. The Apostle says: ". . . who for the joy set before Him, endured a cross." Thus we also ought to do: we need to suffer to attain joy, the true joy, not the false, not the gilded, not the superficial delight of the world, but the real, profound joy that reaches even to the core of our soul, the joy that anoints our hearts definitively. True happiness, true joy, is attained by suffering. Do we not remember that parable of St. Francis of Assisi in which he explained to Brother Leo the true nature of perfect joy? He taught that perfect joy lies not in working prodigies, nor in speaking many languages nor in mastering all sciences, nor in converting the infidel, nor in bringing sinners to the feet of Jesus; true joy consists in suffering for Christ who wanted so ardently to suffer for us.

I do not know if we shall come near understanding this prodigy except by a comparison. We use many things without understanding them. For example, do we know to a fine point the nature of electricity? Are we acquainted with the true explanation of all modern discoveries? We utilize them, nevertheless; they are facts, indisputable facts. Even when we are unable to explain them to ourselves in a satisfactory manner, the facts are still there. Well then, it is a fact that in the spiritual world joy and happiness are found in the very midst of suffering. The saints know this from experience.

St. Thérèse of the Child Jesus said: "I found joy and happiness on earth, but only in suffering." This saint was an innocent girl; neither paradox nor oratorical fancy was suited to her; she said what she felt, she expressed her own personal experience: she found the mysterious, divine phenomenon within her own heart; joy arose from the depths of grief: her only joy, her only happiness came out of her sorrow.

That perfect joy, that unworldly happiness, that mysterious gaiety which we comprehend so faintly, is infused into our heart by the Holy Spirit. He is the only one who can teach us to understand suffering; only He can reveal to us the divine treasures of the cross; He alone possesses the secret of evoking perfect spiritual joy from the deepest sorrow.

Joy of purity, joy of love, joy of sacrifice, — such are the three forms of joy that the Holy Spirit infuses into hearts when He descends to earth.

The Holy Spirit is descending unceasingly; the Christian life as well as the life of the Church is one perpetual Pentecost. When we piously commemorate in a special manner the effusion of the Divine Spirit upon the Apostles in the Cenacle the Spirit of the Lord is poured out upon souls. The whole earth exults with jubilation in spite of fears, dangers and sufferings.

The world is suffering in this our day; everywhere we find reason for fear and for sorrow; but if we are profoundly Christian, in the midst of sorrows and dangers we shall experience within our hearts heavenly joy.

Alleluia! the Spirit of the Lord has been poured out upon the earth; come, let us rejoice and be glad in the Lord! Let us respond to the supernatural joy of Pentecost, deep in our soul. It is a joy, as I have already said, more profound and firm, perhaps, than the joy of the Resurrection, but perhaps also more hidden. Those who live an interior life, those who understand better the mysteries of the Kingdom of Heaven, are keenly sensitive to that perpetual other-worldly gladness.

May the Holy Spirit of the Lord give us that happiness, He who descends upon our souls and effects in them purity, love and sacrifice, so that from these three holy sources may break forth as from a fountain leaping up even to eternal life, the everlasting, holy joy of Pentecost.

FEAST OF THE HOLY TRINITY

O Blessed Trinity

FEAST OF THE HOLY TRINITY

Chapter XII

O Blessed Trinity

"God is charity," said St. John and only God can sound the depths implied in this most simple but most profound statement.

"Look at Me well," advised the Lord to Blessed Angela de Foligno, "do you find in Me anything that is not love?" The mystic adds, "My soul understood conclusively that there is nothing in Him which is not love." Love is the essence of God; love is His life; love is His activity; love is His felicity. Christianity is founded on love for it is nothing else than the participation in God's life condescendingly granted to His creature, — the deification of man.

Love is the law that is condensed into the two great precepts of charity; love is the worship that stems from the Eucharist, the sacrament of love; and love is the doctrine that reveals to us God's mysteries, mysteries of love; the doctrine that illuminates the deep cogitations of man whose greatness is his capacity to love; the doctrine, finally, that describes to us the ladder by which man is elevated from the abyss of his miseries to the blessed height of Eternal Love.

The Mystery of the Trinity, the foundation of Christianity, which contains the essence, the life, the activity, and the happiness of God, is par excellence the mystery of love.

A Lover, the Beloved, and Love—mysterious bond that unites them—is not this the mystery of the august Trinity? The Father and the Son look at each other; They love each other; and the Holy Spirit, infinite, substantial, eternal Love joins Them perpetually. Is this not the mystery of love?

All created love is an imprint and symbol of that eternal love; that which in human love is an inclination (sometimes inconceivable), in God is reality and plenitude. Human love always tends to unity without ever obtaining it fully; it tends toward immortality, forgetting that our affection is ephemeral and inconstant. Divine Love had no beginning, nor will it have end, nor does it admit of change.

Love is fecund because love is divine; and in the august mystery of the Trinity the Father begets the Son, and from the Father and the Son proceeds the Holy Spirit, the infinite, total, and eternal Gift.

True love is sanctity; the blessed sing eternally in praise of the Most Holy Trinity, "Holy, Holy, Holy." Love is felicity; enraptured with admiration and love, the Church never tires of repeating: "O Blessed Trinity!"

The creation is a masterpiece of love because it is the exterior manifestation of God who is love. God sees all things in His Word, in His Beloved, and He loves them in the Word through the Holy Spirit. From the depths of chaos the universe appears, the participation and excess of eternal love living perpetually in the bosom of God. Filled with light, radiant with beauty, the world preserves the impression of the Mystery that produced it as it sings without ceasing the glory of God, the glory of love.

Through supernatural gifts creatures give God greatest glory. Grace, sanctity, glory with the ineffable riches that they comprise, are more than the imitation of eternal love; they are the mysterious participation in the Great Mystery.

The Incarnation is the complement of the Trinity. The latter is the mystery of love within the God-head; the former, the mystery of love that pours itself outward, and by uniting souls with Christ carries them to the most perfect union with God.

"I in them, and Thou in Me, so that we may be consummated in unity," Christ prayed to the Father on the eve of His Passion. These words contain *all*—of time and eternity. The humanity of Christ is the door through which we enter to God, we are united to the Word, we are transformed into the Beloved and we enter the *Mystery of Love.* The Father sees us in the Word, and we see Him in the Word. He loves us and we love Him, and the Holy Spirit unites us. We enter the Mystery of Love . . .

The Trinity is the foundation of the Christian life, of sanctity, of heaven! O Blessed Trinity!

Notes

Part One

Chapter I: THE FEAST OF PURITY

1. Isai. VI, 3.
   Apoc. IV, 8.
   The word "Sanctus" in Greek, "Agios," means "without earth," i.e. "pure." (Editor's note, Spanish edition.)
2. I John, I, 5.
3. Cf. Ps. XXX, 17.
4. John I, 9.
5. II Peter I, 4.
6. Gal. II, 20.
7. Ps. LXXXVI, 1.

Chapter II: THE FECUNDITY OF PURITY

1. Sequence of Pentecost.
2. Cf. Chapter I, 1.
3. I Cor. I, 30.
4. II Peter 1, 3, 4.
5. Zach. VI, 12.
6. Ps. LXXXIX, 4.
7. Apostles Creed.
8. James V, 18.
9. Ps. LXXXIX, 4.
10. I Cor. IV, 15.
11. Gal. IV, 19.
12. Phil. I, 7.
13. *Ibid.* IV, 1.
14. II Cor. XI, 29.
15. Matt. XV, 14.
16. Luke XI, 28.
17. Book IV, Ch. 49, on Luke XI.

Cf. *Roman Breviary in English,* Benziger.

CHAPTER III: THE OBLATION OF PURITY

1. Preface for feasts of Blessed Virgin.
2. Luke II, 32.
3. Cant. II, 2.
4. Luke I, 29.

CHAPTER IV: THE IMMOLATION OF PURITY

1. Isai. LIII, 6.
2. II Cor. V, 21.
3. Ps. XVII, 6.
4. This was written before the Order of Holy Week was restored.
5. We would now say commemorates: no longer a feast.
6. Cf. *Sequence "Stabat Mater."*
7. In the Office of Tenebrae fifteen candles are lighted in a large triangular candelabrum. The candles are gradually extinguished, one after the other, at the close of each psalm, except the highest which always remains lighted.
8. Hymn of Easter Vespers. Cf. *A Short Breviary,* W. Heidt, O.S.B.

CHAPTER V: THE TRIUMPH OF PURITY

1. Easter Sequence. Cf. *St. Andrew Daily Missal.*
2. *Ibid.*
3. *Ibid.*
4. Hymn of Lauds for Sundays in Lent. Cf. *Roman Breviary in English,* Benziger.
5. Cant. II, 11-13.
6. Rom. VIII, 38-39.
7. Antiphon of Easter-tide.

CHAPTER VI: THE EFFUSION OF PURITY

1. John XVI, 7.
2. Heb. IX, 12.
3. *Epliklesis* in Ordinary of Mass.
4. John IV, 14.
5. John VII, 38-39.
6. *Ibid.*
7. Sequence of Pentecost. Cf. *St. Andrew Daily Missal.*
8. These pages were written when the religious persecution in Mexico had suspended religious worship.

CHAPTER VII: THE FOUNTAIN OF PURITY

1. Isai. XLV, 8.
2. Ps. LXXXIV, 11.
3. Col. II, 3.
4. Cf. I John I, 1.
5. Preface of Nativity.
6. Ascension Communicantes.
7. Cant. V, 16.
8. John XIX, 35.
9. *Ibid.*, 34.
10. Cf. Matt. XIII, 52.
11. Bul. "Ineffabilis Deus."
12. Hymn at Matins, feast of Mary, Mediatrix of All Graces. Cf. *Roman Breviary in English,* Benziger.

CHAPTER VIII: THE CONSUMMATION OF PURITY

1. Cf. Christmas Preface.
2. Phil. III, 20.
3. Cf. Cant. III, 4.
4. Cf. Holy Saturday Liturgy — Blessing of Paschal Candle.
5. I.Q. XII, art. 1.
6. Luke I, 33.
7. Ps. CXIX, 5.
8. II IIae. Q. XXIV, art. 9.
9. Ps. XLIV, 14.
10. John XIV, 27.

CHAPTER IX: THE PERFECTION OF PURITY

1. Cant. VIII, 6.
2. I Cor. V, 8.
3. John I, 17.
4. Cf. Acts VI, 3.
5. Cf. Phil. III, 20.

PART TWO

CHAPTER I: KEY OF DAVID

1. Isai. XXII, 22.
   Apoc. III, 7.
   Luke I, 79.
   This is one of the seven Greater Antiphons with which the Church prepares for the birth of the Infant God. They are sung with a special solemnity during Vespers on the seven days preceding Christmas.
2. Matt. XVI, 19.
3. Rom. VII, 38-39.

CHAPTER II: THE MYSTERY OF WEAKNESS

1. Luke II, 12.
2. John I, 14.
3. Phil. II, 7.
4. Cf. *"Adoro Te Devote."*
5. II Cor. XIII, 10.
   "For when I am weak, then I am strong," that is, the secret of my strength is in my weakness.
6. *Ibid.*
7. Wis. III, 2, 3.

CHAPTER III: SORROW AND JOY

1. Prov. XIV, 13.
2. Matt. XVI, 21-23.
3. Reference to apparition of Our Lady of Guadalupe.
4. Archbishop Martinez wrote this chapter during the persecution of the Church in Mexico.
5. John XVI, 33.

CHAPTER IV: PERFECT JOY

1. I John IV, 16.
2. John III, 29.
3. John VIII, 49-50.
4. Luke X, 21.
5. I John III, 9.
6. Cf. Cant. I, 1.
7. *Op. cit.,* Ch. IV, Part One, Note 6.

CHAPTER V: ALLELUIA

1. John XV, 11.
2. *Ibid.* XVI, 24.
3. *Ibid.* XVII, 13.

CHAPTER VI: EASTER GLADNESS

1. Phil. IV, 4.
2. This was written before the restoration of the Easter Vigil.

CHAPTER VIII: COME, HOLY SPIRIT

1. Apoc. XXII, 17.
2. Eccles. XXIV, 29.
3. Dan. X, 11.
4. Wis. VII, 7.
5. Ps. LXXX, 11.
6. Matt. V, 6.
7. Wis. VI, 21.

CHAPTER X: THE PARACLETE

1. John XIV, 16.
2. *Ibid.,* 26.
3. *Veni, Sancte Spiritus.*
4. Ps. LXXXIII, 4.
5. John XIV, 23.
6. John XIV, 6.
7. John XVII, 22, 23.
8. Rom. V, 5.
9. Wis. III, 2, 3.
10. *Veni, Sancte Spiritus.* Cf. *St. Andrew Daily Missal.*

CHAPTER XI: SOURCES OF JOY

1. Heb. XII, 2.
2. Ps. XCIV, 1.
3. Cf. Ps. CXIV, 3. Cf. Mark XVI, 34. Ps. XVII, 6.
   Ps. XVII, 6.
4. II Cor. VII, 4.
5. I Peter IV, 13.